SOCCER GAMES

Fun Activities for Ages 4 to 12

by Andrew Caruso

REEDSWAIN PUBLISHING

**Library of Congress
Cataloging - in - Publication Data**

Soccer Games: Fun Activities for Ages 4 to 12
by Andrew Caruso

ISBN-13: 978-1-59164-235-0
Library of Congress Control Number: 2014959393
© 2014

Diagrams created using easy Sports-Graphics Software
www.easy-sports-graphics.com

Art Direction, Layout and Proofing
Bryan R. Beaver

Reedswain Publishing
88 Wells Road
Spring City, PA 19475
www. reedswain.com
orders@reedswain.com

TABLE OF CONTENTS

Dedicated to all the volunteer coaches who give their time to youth to foster their development in soccer, sportsmanship, healthy exercise, fun and character development.

In order to have adequate game oriented activities for novice coaches, high level coaches (clinicians, licensing instructors, coaching directors, etc.) can advise or issue the volunteers they instruct to have this book.

Administrators should ensure that new volunteers at least receive a preparatory clinic, balls, cones, vests and printed material such as this book so they can provide enjoyable and valuable soccer learning experiences for their eager youngsters. It is the barest minimum that programs should provide to those who volunteer their time.

If coaches can spend 75 plus hours in a season, it would seem sensible that they spend at least two hours in a clinic in order to have a program that children learn from and enjoy. Activities that are fun and truly teach the game will bring the children back to the game in future seasons. Why not spend two hours to make the other 75 hours truly meet the needs of the children!

This book goes well beyond merely prescribing innumerable motivating games that teach an enormous amount of soccer. Appropriate coaching methods are integrated into the technical/tactical exercises. However, at first just learn these valuable activities and later on the finer points of coaching youth soccer.

PREFACE

This text is written for novice coaches and therefore explanations are very detailed, simple and clear. Many clinicians, coaching directors, licensing instructors and other experienced coaches might use the text for activities when teaching coaches of ages 4-11. In any case there may be many items that can be useful to the experienced soccer coach. The explicit detail may be a reminder of details needed when providing instruction for the novice soccer coach.

While novices will benefit most from a complete reading, it might be used as a reference for those instructing beginning coaches.

This is an excellent text as a follow up reminder of useful activities for novices.

Instilling a love of the game is the most important factor because if the player does not develop a passion for the game he/she will not engage in the numerous hours of personal individual play that is required to develop a highly competent player. Certainly for many the main goal is a healthy body with a mind of quality values. Certainly, building character and good sportsmanship is a worthy goal of any youth program. Nonetheless all those values and hard work to achieve excellence must be incorporated, as those habits are life long assets.

There just may be that youngster who will consider soccer as an avenue for a college scholarship or professional career. But without playing on their own it is close to impossible to attain the very high level of skill required for such aspirations. Self initiated practice, playing on one's own, is different because instead of the coach, the child is the creator, the 'visualizer', and nothing can match the power of that form of learning. To even be a good high school or college player one must practice on one's own.

Motivating the child through fun learning games is the best chance a coach has to provide the basis for self motivated learning in young players.

INTRODUCTION

The basics of quality youth coaching are to ensure abundant ball contact through fun games that teach soccer skills. The abundant touches are accomplished first by every child having a ball. Any lines and extended talking denies numerous ball contacts and therefore interferes with the child's soccer development. Line drills naturally deprive the players of the necessary ball touches required for their development.

Running laps is also unnecessary, because when playing children run as hard as they can and then rest. This constitutes the highest level of fitness called interval training. The beauty is that children do this, and it is 100% individualized so that nothing we can do will be superior to that form of fitness. In addition, it is the most economical form of training, since playing embodies technique, tactics and fitness.

The second critical element is actually playing the game. At young ages the playing is in 1v1 and shortsided games. Almost invariably there is a goal, target or a place to get to. It could be hitting a cone, crossing an endline, an actual goal, but there is a specific destination.

To clarify the ball contact, approximately 800 plus touches must take place in a session, and competitive games of great variety must consume two thirds or more of the session. While this is easy to say, it requires the coach to possess many fun game activities, and thus the necessity for this book.

To accumulate the experience of knowing the hundreds of fun activities, methods, and games would be a monumental task. Here the entire process is done for you, and you can pick the most useful to your purposes. Also, because the games are specified by skill domain in the table of contents, one need not peruse an entire book to find a given type of skill.

What drives people from coaching, or causes them to not even consider volunteering initially is the insufficiency of assistance offered to the parent volunteer. Many programs don't even provide cones and vests to new volunteer coaches. Supplying balls is even more rare. The demand for being educated for coaching and the provision of actual material for performing the task is even more rare. Soccer programs must provide clinics and printed material such as this book. The idea that they end up with no coaches due to such requirements is a total fallacy, because the programs that require volunteer coaches to attend clinics have just as many and even more coaches and they have them for longer periods of time. Why? Because when a volunteer does the coaching correctly it is more enjoyable because they can clearly see player growth.

Stated in even simpler terms, the ball is the first teacher, the game is the second teacher and the coach is the third teacher, and as long as the third teacher does not deny the first and second 'teachers' they will do a good job of encouraging the children to play this great game. If the children do not touch the ball in great abundance there is little chance for them to acquire the ball control and other skills of the game. The number of skills ranges in the hundreds, from simple dribbling and receiving and passing to complex power instep drive, heading, flicks, chipping, combination play and more. Maybe the simplest expression of quality youth coaching is being certain to ensure that the ball and the game do the vast bulk of the teaching. This is done by designing an activity that teaches the desired skill, which is exactly what this book does.

The late Mike Berticelli, former head coach of men's soccer at Notre Dame, listed the most common errors of youth coaching as positional play, drills, over coaching, training the team and assessing success through wins. One could add running without the ball, lengthy talks, and forcing passing instead of admiring early stages of dribbling skills. The antidotes for positions are all forms of shortsided play from 1v1 to 2v1, through 4v4. At an advanced level, an understanding of team shape vs positional play. To replace drills and lines, competitive games will increase learning and motivation. For over-coaching keep the ball and activities as the centerpiece of your sessions. To avoid training the team constantly, be mindful of players' individual development. Of course the real poison is the winning mania taking precedence over the child's skill progress. It is difficult to not give in to the misguided parents who think that winning an eight year old game is the equivalent of winning the World Cup. Maybe a clear definition of cheering is in order. Calling a specific child's name or a player with the ball is coaching, not cheering. This could be clarified at the beginning of the season parent meeting. Also, yelling out instructions to players is not cheering, it is coaching and is not the role of parent spectators.

There can be the development of a "technique freak" who cannot make reasonably good tactical decisions if technique is all that is taught. However, the restricted game playing and the unrestricted game playing will not allow that to happen, since playing always involves the child's own decision making. Thus, the early stages of tactics, in the unrestricted play, is in the control of the player, which initiates decision making (tactics). This ensures the child's ownership of his game, creativity and tactical development. At a later age, more small group tactics (combination play, third man-on, etc.) and team tactics will play a bigger role, although even professional teams spend time on technical maintenance and development, especially during the warm-up phase of training.

The single 'tactic' that coaches must constantly keep in mind is that when the ball is mindlessly kicked to nowhere, correction is needed. This tendency of mindless kicking must be deterred even before it becomes a habit.

As far as psychology is concerned, simply be positive; find the good things children do. Appreciate a child's joy when he/she goes from one juggle and catch to two continuous juggles. Find great joy when the child takes on and beats an opponent. By the same token, take joy when the defender wins the ball from an attacker. Appreciate the smiles when they lift the ball or complete a pass. Celebrate the 3 goals in the game lost 5 to 3. Defense is really something that only begins to be of concern once they have the offensive skills of dribbling, collection, passing, etc. After all, at the young ages players lose the ball more than the other team wins the ball. Mindful passes that have an intended receiver but fail to reach a teammate must be congratulated instead of causing dismay. The renowned former United States National Women's Soccer Coach Tony DiCicco said it best, "Catch Them Being Good", which is also the title of his book.

Often included in the domain of psychology is the area of goal setting. Many players and coaches think that a worthy goal is to be an All Star or league champions, etc. This is called an outcome goal and while there is nothing wrong with this, it is ancillary to performance goals. Performance goals are daily, weekly and seasonal goals with specificity that are the essence of achieving positive outcomes. Performance goals are such things as: "Today I am going to perfect my changes of direction". This is accompanied by where, when, how many repetitions and other details of how I am going to accomplish this. An example might be: "I will go to practice 30 minutes early, and use the Pullback and Scissor turns at least 50 times each". Having these performance goals on a regular basis for specific skills that one wants to develop is really what allows players to be whatever they desire, whether it be a starter on the team, an All Star, the high scorer or whatever.

Outcome goals without performance goals are of little value. Outcome goals supported by regular detailed performance goals are the essence of what all high level achievers do. Outcome goals are sometimes referred to as Dream Goals, and as long as they are not accompanied by performance goals, that's all they are!

While there is much to be accomplished by the coach and/or player in the domain of sports psychology, the concept of **focus** looms very high on the list of priorities. The two main tenants of focus are: 1) remain in the here and now 2) be certain you are having positive thoughts of previous experiences. The positive thoughts do not necessarily have to be in the realm of your sport experience, but can be any positive life experience you have had. Although research has not yet separated specific positive sports experiences from general life experiences as being the most valuable, it would seem that those positive experiences related to the activity in progress would be of greater value.

As a coach, in very basic terms, attempt to have four positive comments for every correction you make. Away from the folly of Hollywood and "One for the Gipper" speeches, even the highest level coaches are much more positive than admonishing. How can we who deal with young enthusiastic learners constantly focus only on correcting them? Leave the admonishing coaches and the exciting "One for the Gipper" speeches to the Hollywood screen. Furthermore, our work with individuals greatly exceeds any discussions that address the whole team.

These young age groups, more so than older children, require more than one coach. There are enough people who will help if the head coach truly desires help. A one man show denies individual attention and causes time wasting when injuries or TLC is necessary for one of the players. Necessary parent pick up, illness, unforeseen emergencies and many other factors occur. With multiple coaches there is no interruption or loss of motivation or ball touches due to such occurrences. As a former consultant to a large soccer program, I consistently noted better sessions where two or more coaches were involved with very young players, irrespective of the experience and ability of the lead coach. Also, the younger, less experienced coaches who attended the clinics given by the coaching director did better sessions than experienced coaches who used methods geared to older players. Clearly, I would not have predicted this prior to having the opportunity to merely observe and make recommendations to the coaching director of more than twelve U-6 teams (over 1500 players in the total program). So, get an assistant. Females tend to have a bit more experience with these young age levels, so don't avoid that aspect of experience.

Needless to say, clinics, licensing courses, and media instruction for this age level in soccer will all help to complement the activities detailed in this text. Unfortunately, high level licenses are of little value to these young players, unless they were courses specifically for youth players. The major advantage of vast playing experience is that those individuals generally progress faster once given instruction on how to help young developmental players.

Soccer tactics resemble ice and field hockey, basketball, polo, lacrosse and other continuous motion team sports. Therefore, adults in the USA are often somewhat familiar with the tactics long before they learn the specific techniques of soccer. Concepts such as wall passes, takeovers, skip passes, quick counter attack and overlaps (simulated in basketball as a fast break or in American football as a deep receiver) are all somewhat understood. Unfortunately, early stages must be dominated by technique and individual skill development, not team instruction and formations.

While it may seem that youth coaching requires a great deal of knowledge, in actuality it mostly requires patience, a very positive outlook and enjoying the day by day minor accomplishments that add up to significant progress over a period of time. The satisfaction of the significant accomplishments of the children and the knowledge that you were the facilitator of that growth offers joys beyond one's initial understanding.

Unfortunately, age designations poorly represent the individual abilities of young players. Thus, the age designations are only a crude representation. Clearly a ten year old who has been enrolled in soccer since age five and has been playing on his own may be very different than a ten year old who is being introduced to the game for the first time. Thus the coach must make her own judgments when choosing appropriate activities. In any case it is always best to start at an easy level, possibly a review level before entering a level of new learning. With some adaptation, most of these activities can be used with the entire age level, with many even appropriate to older players.

Many of the activities enumerated are very good for different purposes than listed here. This only goes to further indicate that it is a valuable activity that accomplishes more than a single objective. In the broadest sense, when an activity does more than one of the following: technical, tactical, fitness and psychology, we refer to that as economical training, which is generally considered a positive. Of course, all match games and almost all of the innumerable playing games listed also address all four basics of the game. Due to the large array of activities, choose those that your players enjoy and reuse them regularly.

Whenever it is not going well just move to playing the game. There is nothing that we can do as coaches of young players that is more valuable than playing the game. Most of us never give the players enough unrestricted playing and yet games are the most important part of learning to be a good player. How can you be prepared to play a game if the only thing you ever do is have soccer instruction? This is especially true if that instruction is drills instead of games. Manny Schellscheidt, a true icon of U.S. soccer, once said to me, "Drills are for military, games are for football (soccer)."

Transfer of learning from drills to the actual games is low; a bit better for soccer games, but nothing surpasses unrestricted playing! Of course if it is shortsided it also has the advantage of many ball touches and more tactical decision making. It also is very rigorous so that fitness is taken care of. If youngsters have fun they will be very competitive in those shortsided games and thus even mental toughness is developed. That covers all the needs of developing a good soccer player.

You will see many activities with names you never heard of. This is because I often name an activity after the person I learned it from. Sometimes this helps to remember the activity and gives an ounce of credit to those who have helped my growth in coaching. Hopefully, much of that learning can be received by you.

A very simplified training session starts with everyone with a ball making moves, changing speed and changing directions, etc. for roughly 15 minutes. This is followed by instruction of the day with trials without defense (10 minutes), move to more speed and/or defense (10 minutes), use the instructional item in a restricted game (15 minutes), move to free play (25 minutes). Be flexible in the amount of time according to the age level, but always attempt to have most of the time in playing with the free play being at minimum one third of the session.

Enjoy!

BASICS OF BASICS

Basics of Basics are the areas of soccer coaching that we do not necessarily do any progressions of, but we insist on these items in everything we do. These are:

- In every exercise players should not strike dead balls to initiate play; instead they should take a preparatory touch before striking the ball. Why? Because balls prepared properly nearly always result in good passes, services, crosses or shots. Poor preparatory touches invariably have a poor result. Obviously, corner kicks, directs, kickoffs, goal kicks etc. are an exception.
- In every exercise we do not tolerate not going to the ball. Why? Because when this is done in the actual game the defender usually wins the ball.
- Goal side defending must also be consistently enforced.
- More difficult to establish is collecting away from pressure instead of straight forward.
- Opening the hips in simpler terms means facing as many teammates and opponents as possible in order to make a good decision. Good decisions are highly unlikely when near a sideline and facing directly at the sideline or where neither teammates nor opponents are in the player's vision. Open hips generally means side-on facing to the penetration (goal) direction.
- Defensive stance is low, knees bent, eyes on the ball, feet shoulder width apart, balls of the feet the main surface touching the ground and in the final approach the player must move slowly with small steps.
- Never pass up shots from a reasonable distance with a chance to score. Shoot when a shot is available. Avoid unnecessary touches and movement to poor angle locations in relation to goal.
- Opening up, spreading out, when our team has won the ball or is about to win the ball.
- Pressing the ball, everyone defending, compacting whenever the ball is possessed by the opponent. Stay connected and move as a unit.
- Keeping one's head up whenever possible when dribbling is important.

Although it does not fit in the same class with the above items, it certainly is worth mentioning that when facing one's own goalkeeper and closely marked, attempting to turn and pass is ill advised. With a defender on a player's back, learn to make an excellent pass to the keeper or if that is not possible play the ball safely out-of-bounds. Mostly for age ten and up.

Also while not a Basic of Basics for ages 4-12, we offer many reminders to collect a ball cleanly, not lifting it so that time goes by allowing the defense time to win the ball or allowing the ball to spray 4+ yards away. By the same token, trapping a ball dead so that it requires lowering the head to see where it is is nothing but a bad habit. For more than three decades we have been using the term "collecting" the ball instead of the old verbiage of "trapping" the ball because the modern game demands a faster speed of play, and collecting away from pressure allows time and space.

Granted, on occasion a progression on some of the Basic of Basics can be appropriate, especially for ages 4-8, but occasional progressions will not change careless behavior if it is constantly allowed while playing in game situations in training or matches. Frequent personal reminders in training might instill the correct behavior.

Certainly this is a wonderful area for an assistant coach to take a player individually and work on one of these bad habits. By the same token, the head coach can take a youngster either before or after practice to alleviate one of these negative habits. It is especially important, when possible, to point out the specific technical error and how a positive use of the skill will help the player and the team. For the early ages it might be best to focus on how it will help them personally. For an older youngster, once they reach the peer pressure concerns (ages 12 and above), explaining how it will help the team can be appropriate.

Trying to keep these basics in mind and the use of frequent reminders in training is a good idea. Better still, compliment youngsters when they do these things well. In games against opponents, reminders are not to be used as it distracts from the game and the players' enjoyment and likely reduces the chances of success. During games the coach's constant commentary is nothing more than therapy for the coach. Players are not there for the coach, they are there for their enjoyment. We as coaches should be there for the player's enjoyment and personal growth. Observe, commit to memory, and attempt to improve the skills in training sessions.

DRIBBLING

Dribbling is the foundation of all player development and eventual success in the game. Not only is winning 1v1 battles important, but the passing/receiving game requires quality dribbling since there are numerous times when no pass is available. In these instances, shielding and moving with the ball (dribbling) to find an open crease to pass through is a necessity. Of course preparing a ball for long ball service or distant shots also requires deft ball preparation dribbling. Quality ball control dribbling allows the player to get his head up and use his vision to make good decisions. Thus, this first section and the beginning of almost all practice sessions with youth players begin with each having their own ball and dribbling abundantly.

The general essence of dribbling is change of direction and change of speed, both of which must be emphasized throughout all of the instruction. Strangely, the hard part with young players is to get them to go slow so that a change in speed is possible. The main way to accomplish this is to have the players touch the ball with every step they take, make the move and accelerate. The last motion of a move is simultaneously THE BEGINNING OF THE ACCELERATION. Do not allow moves to be made and then subsequently the acceleration as that allows the defender to negate the deception of the move! The dribbling move and acceleration is one continuous movement as opposed to a move, a hesitation, and then acceleration. There are occasions when a dribbler freezes a defender on purpose.

The late Dr. Tom Fleck, sort of the father of the realm of targeting age appropriate soccer activities for youth in the U.S., would introduce the very young children to the game and the coach by merely taking their ball and tossing it about 20 yards for them to return to him. Some of his many commands for each round of retrieval were: Return the ball to me (the coach) by carrying the ball using your hands, bounce the ball once and catch it repeatedly, toss and catch the ball, crawl on the ground and use your knees to advance the ball, crawl and use your head, dribble slowly trying to touch the ball with every step and return it, repeatedly make short rolls of the ball on the ground and then pick the ball up, dribble back to me at speed, etc. The distance the ball is thrown varies according to the ability of the child. Every given instruction was demonstrated for simplicity and assurance of success. This activity introduces the children to following simple commands and gets them familiar with the ball. General commands such as "touch the ball with the inside of the foot" help the dribbling phase. All voice commands are demonstrated until players know exactly what they are.

Another stage in various voice commands while every player has a ball is to introduce use of all the foot surfaces and dribbling moves. This is often done for all the ages focused on in this text. All instructions are demonstrated for a few seconds.

Basic

Basic is simply touching the ball to the insides of both feet in rapid succession. It allows many touches of the ball in a short period of time. It incorporates balance and is fundamental to such things as the push pass, receiving and some moves to beat a defender.

- Touch the ball with the inside of both feet in rapid succession
- Touch the ball only with the outside of your foot; both feet
- Walk with the ball (dribbling) attempting to touch the ball with every step you take
- Touch the ball with the sole of the foot: progress to touch the ball with the sole of both feet in rapid succession---this has a sort of hop to it.

Toe Taps

Toe taps help improve balance, facilitate fast footwork and develop basic ball control. They are commonly used in dribbling and one on one moves. They are a favorite technique of Cristiano Ronaldo.

Using the sole of the foot see if you can move the ball slowly backwards; forward; sideways; one command at a time at early stages.

Hit the Ball

See if you can hit someone else's ball; when you get 5 hits go down on one knee; declare the first, second and third winners and start a new round; 4 to 6 rounds is probably about right

By trying to hit someone else's ball one must use vision, turn away to protect one's ball, react quickly, be aware of open spaces and most of all compete to be the first to hit other players' balls 5 times.

When the coach calls out "Exchange!" change balls with other members of the group; stop your ball with the sole of the foot before seeking another ball, then continue dribbling with the newly acquired ball. Eventually this becomes 'musical chairs' with the one without a ball required to retrieve a ball sent by the coach about 20 yards out of the grid area.

Touch em All

Spread about 12 cones in an area about 15 yards square and ask the players to dribble and touch each cone with their ball as quickly as they can. First to touch all cones wins. Best to cajole cheaters, rather than serious admonishment. Nonetheless, observe carefully and simply tell a false winner which cone she missed.

Hitting all the cones first means good ball control, head up to see open cones, control with speed and fires competitive instincts.

Feint kicking the ball hard and then just touch it past another player or to open space for a speed dribble; have players accentuate feinting. Sometimes it is necessary to explain that feinting, the term used in soccer, means to perform a fake move. Feinting must be taught, as it is a very important skill. Coaches must constantly emphasize it, . Dribbling, passing and shooting often require quality feints in order to achieve a player's true intention!

Another move is to push the ball past someone and run around the opposite side. This works because the defender invariably tries to block the dribbler from the ball on the side that he was beaten; thus going the other way is often the shortest route to the ball. While the defender must turn, the dribbler facing the ball is at an advantage. Especially if the ball pushed past the defender is the first step to the ball, the dribbler has a good chance of success.

'The Cruyff move' simply has the player take the ball behind the standing foot with the inside of the other foot. Requires standing foot in front of the ball and standing knee well bent with body weight leaning forward for balance. Use of hands for balance also helps.

'Pulling a V' is putting your right foot on the ball and pulling it back to yourself at an angle and then taking off going right with the outside of the foot or going left with the inside of the foot. Use the same motions with the left foot.

A 'sideways sole roll' generally across the body followed by a touch forward with acceleration is another move----popularized by Ronaldo of Real Madrid.

'The Maradona' is a move in which while going forward the player steps to the side of the ball with both feet, makes a 180^0 turn without the ball, and then sole rolls the ball forward turning another 180^0 while continuing to dribble in the same general direction.

'Swivel hips' is nothing more than throwing the hips in an exaggerated fashion in one direction and then taking the ball in the opposite direction; most effective with the outside of the foot.

'The Charlton' move might be the simplest, yet extremely effective move. The player touches the ball to the left with the inside of the right foot and rapidly touches the ball in the opposite direction with the outside of the same foot, mostly using the toe area of the boot. Also outside/inside, outside/inside/ outside and other variations thereof.

The outside of the foot controlled ball touching is useful for deceptive dribbling, long pass, reverse banana passes, receiving as to keep the defender far from the ball and of course for shooting.

Another voice command that can be used while all players are dribbling in a grid is "Groups of Three!". On this call players quickly arrange themselves in groups of three. Those who do not make it to a correct number group or who are very late in doing so must do 10 toe taps.

Moves: Do all with both the dominant and non-dominant foot/leg. Consider about 20 repetitions or segments of about 20 to 30 seconds. Research indicates about 20 repetitions is necessary for establishing a degree of permanence in the realm of motor development.

Heads Up!

Coach has players dribbling in a grid and puts up X number of fingers in the air and players are expected to call out the number. Clearly this is an attempt to get the players to dribble with their heads up in order to improve their vision in an actual game. Change the number about every five seconds, but be unpredictable and vary the time from 3 to 10 seconds. Keep pointing out who has their head up and IS DRIBBLING and correcting those who have their heads down or simply are not really dribbling with the ball. Encourage changes of direction, head turned while dribbling away from the coach. All who are making a serious effort should be recognized.

The emphasis here is dribbling ball control with head up to increase vision! This group is displaying the skill exceptionally well.

Because most moves involve a change in direction, it is also valuable to spend some time on direct instruction of changing direction. Four main turns are:

Sole Roll Pull Turn: This is exactly what it says. Just have the player place his foot on the ball and pull it while turning the body 180°, always facing the ball. The tendency of players is to turn away from the ball. A simple instruction to help correct this behavior is to ask the players to see the ball for the entire movement. Some sources call this "Bye, Bye".

The Sole Roll can also be used as a simple dribbling move with a pullback of the ball and then accelerating again to lose the defender.

Cruyff Turn: Have the player change direction 180° by having one foot move the ball behind the standing leg. If necessary use a line of the field to help the players understand the move's directional change. This is also used to blow by a defender. Requires bent standing leg, weight forward.

Chop: This technique is very effective, especially when the ball changes direction 180°. Allow the ball to go beyond the entire body and legs and then reach out for it with the laces. Ask for ten or more chops in succession, going alternately right and left. Again, sometimes doing this on the line of the field will get the players to make a complete 180° change of direction.

The chop really changes the direction sharply/quickly and can very effectively loses a defender.

Play With Scissors!

The Scissor Move simply has the player move the foot around the ball and then take the ball in a different direction with the same or other foot; generally the most effective is the use of the outside of the other foot. To maintain best body balance, scissor moves are made from the inside to the outside. Put simply, a right footed player using her right foot goes clockwise around the ball.

The scissor move is very commonly used to get past the defender:

Closely allied to turn moves is $360°$ change of direction by simply having players dribble around a cone, mostly using the outside of the foot. Do this with both feet; generally right foot is clockwise, left is counter clockwise. Of course no cone is needed after players learn the $360°$ turn.

In time many different angle directions will be used with the turns in accordance to the game situation, but if players can make the $180°$ turn all the others will be relatively easy. All of these moves can be done to a cone, pole, the coaches, or pretending to take-on one another in a grid. Do all using both feet.

Follow the Leader

Often referred to as **Siamese**, this is another fun dribbling activity. The follower merely mimics all the moves of the leader. Change leaders about every 45 seconds. Try to maintain a close distance between the two players. If necessary, ask leaders to slow down a bit so the Siamese player can keep up. Good for vision development. Siamese can also be played side by side in order to increase the visual demands.

Here some players are performing extremely well while some others have lost their leader. The key to this activity is in the beginning make certain the leader goes slowly, yet changes direction sharply and frequently and that all players remain in the grid. The head turning is an added benefit.

Snake Fashion Leader usually starts with the coach as the leader of the whole team. It is best done by going around objects such as poles, goals, trees, bleachers or whatever, otherwise the back of the snake traverses very short distances, losing its effectiveness. Move to a creative player being the leader.

The Cage

Have a 10 yard grid with equal number of players along each mid side of the grid. All have a ball and they simply cross the grid from one side to the opposite side continuously. They must cross the entire grid and evade each other. Instill good sharp turns throughout the entire activity. Progress to one defender who attempts to win a ball. If a ball is won the attacker takes the place of the defender and the defender becomes a dribbler. There is no stoppage of dribbling across the grid as the exchange takes place. Players have all kinds of reasons for stopping play, as coaches we must get them in the habit of continuous play because almost all of soccer is continuous play. The whistle means "Go!" not stop. Lax moments during games cause goals to be scored against teams. This habit of quick transition leads to proper transition behavior in games, hopefully for their entire playing careers.

The cage is great for abundant ball contact, head up vision development, stops and changing direction.

Soccer Golf

Have the youngsters dribble and hit the fence, pole, both sides of a goal, a garbage can, the coach's equipment bag, the bench on the side of the field, or whatever objects exist for possible targets. First player to complete the course wins. In between the more exotic targets you can place large cones so that there are nearly "18 holes".

Fish Bowl

Hit the balls of players crossing a grid. Grid is roughly 8 by 16 yards. Two players, one outside each of the long sides of the grid, try to hit a ball of the dribblers who are dribbling from one end to the other and back again. When a dribbler's ball is hit, he joins the players who are trying to hit balls while the other becomes a dribbler.

Xa and Xb (shooters) are trying to hit the balls of the players going across the grid. If you hit a player's ball you become the dribbler; the player whose ball was hit becomes a shooter. The more balls available simply helps to make the exercise more competitive.

The last player whose ball was never hit wins. Usually the game goes down to 1 or 2 winners. Be certain that players are not waiting beyond the endlines; that is, not dribbling. Not dribbling is a violation. Changing speed and changing direction, always going somewhat forward, is required. Compliment accomplished players who change speed and direction, who hide behind another dribbler so the sideline 'shooters' cannot hit their ball or perform any strategy that helps them win while maintaining the spirit of the game. Sideline players have 3 balls to start with; they get more balls by retrieving balls shot from the opposite side. Adjust the grid width to foster success. If "Shooters" are not successful, have a change in rules so that one must merely hit the player's legs. That will increase the changing of roles. When shooters have no balls all players retrieve all the balls. To end the game simply have everyone whose ball was hit be a "Shooter." Do they ever figure out that working together is more effective? If not, simply ask the question, "How can the "Shooters" improve their success?"

Pick Up the Cones

Have 20-30 cones or any objects such as pieces of cloth, tennis balls or whatever spread over a large portion of the field. After some of the dribbling exercises clarified in this section, have a contest of who can pick up the most cones (pieces of cloth or whatever) and bring them to the coach at the coaching bag/water bottles location. The player with the most objects wins. Young players love contests of all kinds and at the same time valuable fitness training is being accomplished.

obstacle Course Dribbling

Set up 5 to 10 cones for players to dribble around. This aids changes of direction and dribbling control. At ages 10 and above there are many more competitive fun activities more useful than this. But for the 5-7 year olds they get some success in dribbling before facing an opponent. They also gain many touches of the ball and develop confidence with the ball, which is definitely important to young players. A random arrangement involving varied distances provides token reality.

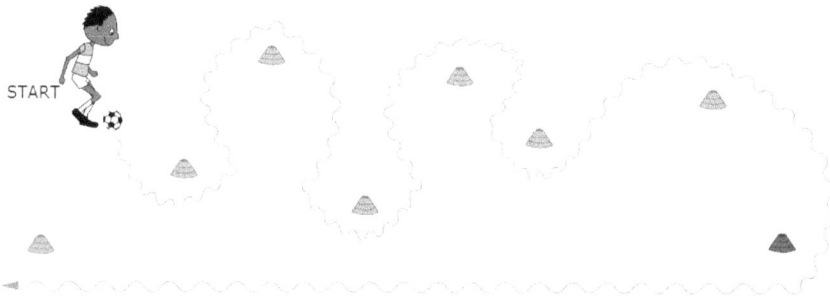

Demand a speed dribble back to the start location after passing the last cone in the obstacle course (cone filled in black). Allow youngsters to pass each other so that all can progress at their appropriate speed (level). Emphasize control above all else. Pairs can make this a relay race. This can be done as a continuous motion exercise.

Red Light, Green Light

Players with a ball are about 25 yards away from the coach in a flat line, usually a line on the field. The coach is facing away from the players and calls "Green Light", which tells the players to dribble forward. When the coach calls out "Red Light", the coach turns, if a child's ball is rolling he must go back to the beginning. Before the game starts the coach shows how to stop a ball by placing your foot on top of the ball. The winner is the first player to end up in line with the coach. At first, turn fast and catch several players at a time so the game has a real challenge to it.

Hit the Coach Under the Knee

A favorite with all groups, mostly for ages 4-10. Use a grid of roughly 20 x 20 yards. Make it an equal challenge to all by actively preventing the superstars from hitting you early and allowing the less skilled players to occasionally hit you under the knee. Strategy for the coach to avoid getting hit is to not always run away from the young charges, but actually go right toward them and pass them before they kick the ball to hit you. In due time assign a player to be the person getting hit, usually one of the better players. Do not be tolerant of youngsters who hit high balls, as this can be dangerous, and is absolutely not in the spirit of the game.

It's hard to believe that these players love their coach when you see the intensity with which they try to hit the him under the knee. No exercise exceeds the fun, effort and ball control that players exhibit when doing this activity.

Win the Balls

Place all the balls in the middle of a square 15 yard grid. For easy management of this activity place all the balls in hula-hoops. Using all players, place equal numbers in the four corners of the grid and on a signal one player from each group goes to get a ball in the middle and dribbles back to their corner. Then the next youngster in the group goes. It makes no difference if some corners have one more or less players than the other groups since only one player at a time from each group is retrieving balls. When all the balls are gone the team with the most balls wins. Multiple winners are fine. Balls are returned to the center by the players dribbling and stopping the ball in the central area. Five rounds are probably about right. If each child has brought a ball to practice and the coach has some extras, use all of them as this activity works best with several balls.

Option: Each corner with players has a ball and one player at a time while dribbling goes to the central area to retrieve a tennis ball (or any object available). The team with the most tennis balls when all balls are gone wins.

Option: Players dribble the tennis balls out of the central area.

This group is really in the spirit of the game.

Straight Tag

While all are dribbling, simply have another dribbling player with a vest in hand go around and tag someone. When they tag someone they throw down the vest, the tagged player picks it up and proceeds to tag someone else. Do not permit players to hand the vest to the tagged player as the game works much better when the vest is thrown to the ground. This is great for dribbling and vision development. Tagging back is not allowed. Larger groups might have two taggers.

Gate Goals

Set up 8 to 10 gate cone goals about 2 yards wide in a random fashion in a 20 yard square grid. Players can start anywhere in the grid. The first option can be the player that dribbles through all gate goals first wins. Follow this by requiring any move or a specific move in front of each gate goal before going through. This environment has dozens of options. Often the final option is two teams, whichever team completes passing through 6 gate goals wins.

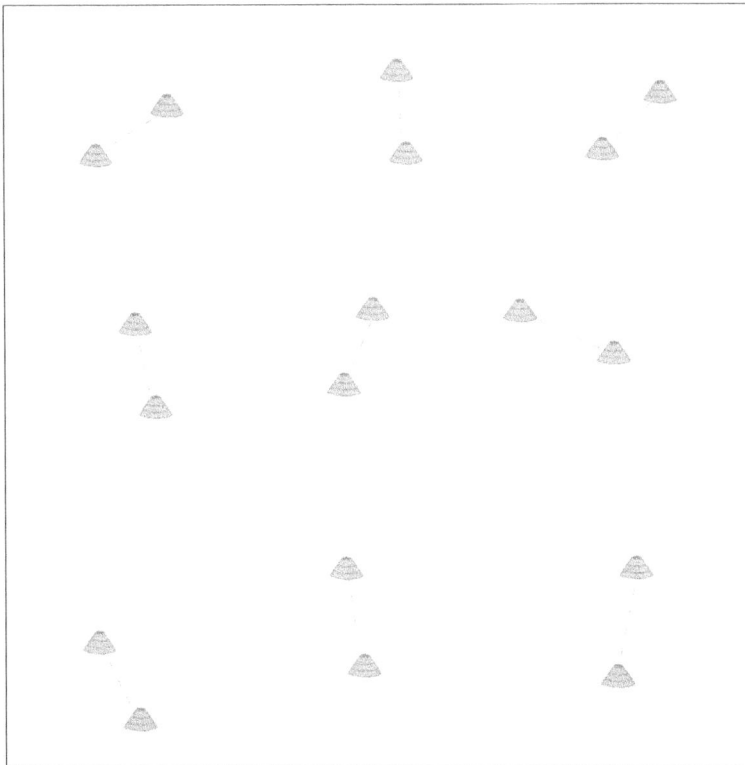

One option for any of the gate goal games is to permit defending, not by goal tending, but allowing players to kick another individual or team's ball out of the grid. Not recommended for starting levels.

Hospital Tag

All the players are dribbling and trying to tag each other. A tagged player places his hand on the tagged body part. After two tags, since there is no third hand, the player must go to the hospital by leaving the grid and doing 20 Basic touches (sending the ball back and forth between the two insides of the feet). Then he returns to the game dribbling. This type of game is called a game of inclusion instead of a game of elimination and this general method is encouraged in all the games played with children. Obviously the players first tagged need the practice more than anyone, so games of elimination are not very productive. Feel free to make up individual rules for superstars such as they must tag others below the knee. They do not see this as punishment, they realize this is a way of creating parity and they appreciate the honor.

Parity is always a desired element in instruction. Anything too simple is boring, anything that is too difficult and cannot be accomplished is frustrating, thus the correct challenge level is called instructional level. As coaches we must always attempt to attain that level for all players at all times for maximum learning value. Individualization is a positive, not a negative.

Hospital Tag: All players dribbling in grid and tagging each other. Clearly a game of inclusion!

Dribbling Relay

In relays we generally use pairs instead of two teams of large numbers to facilitate a greater number of ball touches. Player pairs start from behind a cone and dribble around a cone about 20 feet away. For added ball control dribbling fun, place two cones about 3 feet apart and have the players go around the furthest cone and weave in between the two cones as shown in the diagram. Only one group is shown, but you would have as many setups as you have pairs involved in the relay races. Five to ten repetitions are about right.

Xa has dribbled past the far cone and weaved between the two far cones and then passed to his partner Xb. The first few times make it as simple as go around a single cone and dribble back to partner. At much later stages demand a move be made at the cone. Use your own wrinkles to suit your purpose. Many varied cone arrangements are possible.

Circle Dribbling

Using the center circle of the field or a circle created with cones, one ball for every 3 players, simply have players dribble across the circle and give the ball to a teammate who does likewise. The necessity to avoid collisions with other players forces some changes of speed, changes of direction and visual development. Can also be used for passing/receiving. At higher levels this format is used for juggling, combination moves such as wall passes, heading and many other skills. By simply placing a large cone in the center of the circle, this can be used for turning, demanding a specific turn, and then still giving the ball to a teammate either with a takeover or pass. This format is widely used for warm-ups for varying age levels. Eye contact, properly weighted passes, movement to the ball and communication are often coaching points in these exercises.

Circle Dribbling: It looks like the coach could use a couple more balls so that there are more touches and more fun.

Get Away

Two teams of any number with one team all dribbling balls in a central circle about 10 yards in diameter in a square grid of about 20 x 20 yards. On the coach's signal "Escape", the dribbling team leaves the circle to dribble over any perimeter line of the square grid. The other team is outside the grid and tries to prevent them from getting over any perimeter line of the grid. If they successfully win a ball, they dribble into the circle to score a point. The process is repeated but the roles are reversed. For each round, each team having a chance to dribble from the central area over the grid lines, the winner is the team that won the most balls. When the round is over, balls are dribbled back to the central area unopposed by the team that was defending. Generally, interest remains high for at least 5 rounds.

Option: Every man for himself; whoever wins a ball when the others are dribbling out of the circle goes into the circle as a dribbler for the next round.

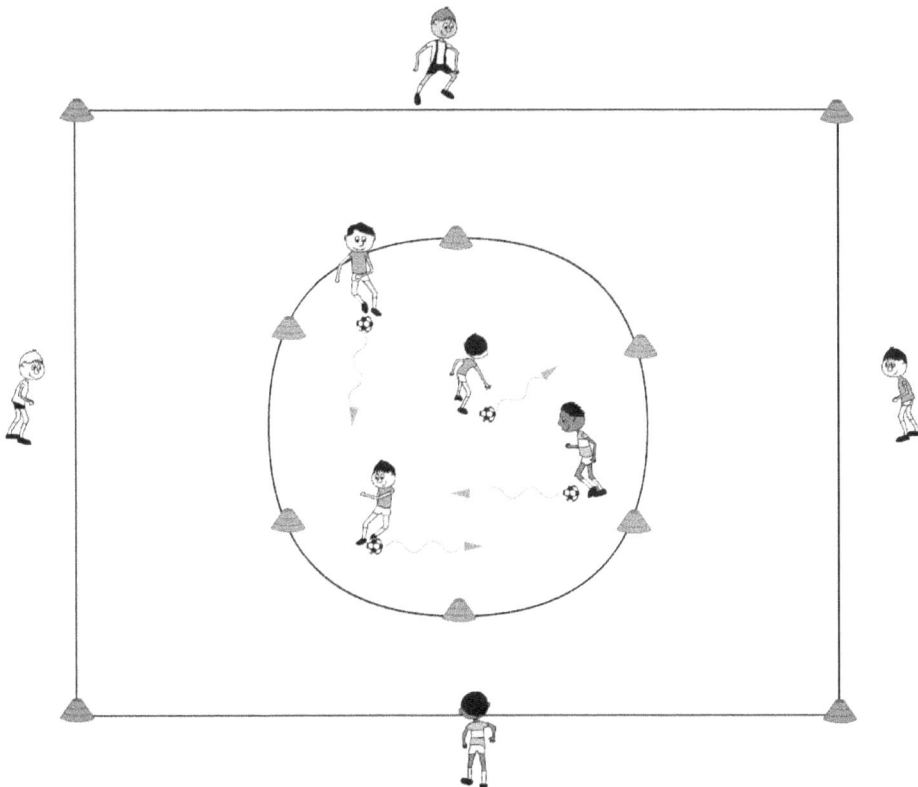

The defenders succeed when they gain control of the ball and dribble into the circle. All of one team is dribbling in the circular area before the escape command is made.

The time between rounds should be brief. Vary the amount of time for calling for the escape group so that all stay attentive in order to establish extended focus time. Leave the defensive organization completely up to the players. Dribbling players will learn that keeping their body between the defender and themselves will yield success. If the offense is too successful, designate only two opposite grid lines for each team to dribble over instead of all 4 sides. To add fitness have the defending group jog around the grid before the escape command.

Tail Tag

An excellent instructional fun dribbling game in a 20 yard square grid. All players have a ball and shirts tucked in shorts and have a vest hanging out of the back of their shorts. The player who gets the most tails from teammates wins. The person with the last tail is also a co-winner. Play 4 or 5 rounds. Compliment self initiated double teaming and other good strategies such as quick turns to move one's tail away from the attacker. This is excellent for all ages. A fringe benefit is you get to see attacking and defending personalities. Attackers often seek to have the most vests; defenders often try to have the last vest.

It's not always this perfect, but the ones still with tails ARE DEFENDERS and the one with the hand full of tails is the midfield attacker.

Safe Areas Tag

All players are dribbling with a vest in their hand. Grid is about 15 yards square. One player is designated as a tagger to start the game. In the safe areas, you cannot be tagged. However, only one player per area is permitted at any given moment. When another player comes into the area the other player must leave. Whenever you get tagged you throw down your vest and become a "Tagger". The last player with a vest wins.

Option: Two permanent taggers and every round change taggers. Try to find your own wrinkles that keep the game fun and competitive and the players interested.

Shown is X entering the area which demands Y leave the area. For six players only have one safe area and add one safe area for every additional two players. The grid shown will accommodate 12 to 18 players. Appropriate for ages 7 to high school.

The game structure teaches dribbling and vision, requires fitness and there is an abundance of decision making required to be successful. Some players will learn that standing near a safe area allows movement into the safe area, thus safety from being tagged. The player in the safe area is vulnerable and will often leave of her own accord. Excellent for all ages.

Cops and Robbers

Cops and Robbers has many forms. One form has the robbers all dribbling in the big grid with a central area grid as the jail. The cops are not dribbling. If a cop wins the ball from a robber, the robber must go in jail. Winning the ball is defined as the cop obtaining the ball making 2 consecutive controlled touches. He then knocks the ball about 15 yards out of the grid and continues to put players in jail. A fellow robber can release a prisoner by passing a ball through the jailed player's legs. When the jailbird is released from jail he sprints to get his ball back and returns to dribbling.

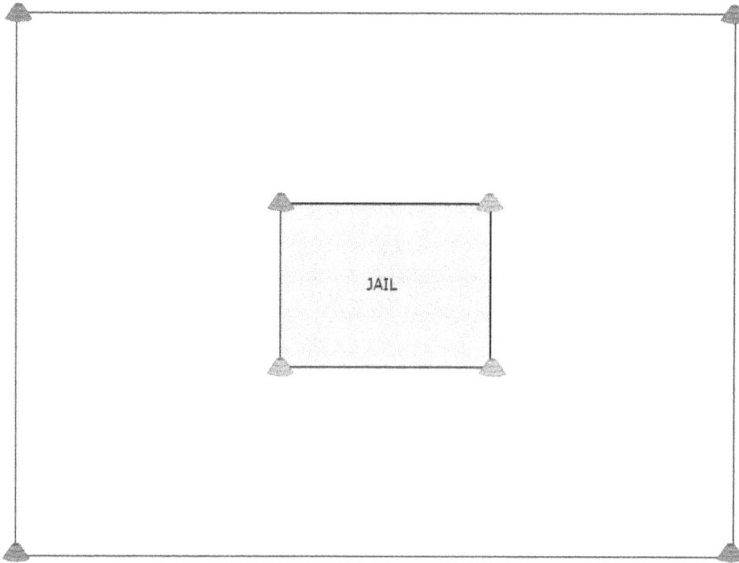

Best to have one or two cops and the rest of the team as robbers. Large grid is 20x20 yards, jail is 5x5 yards.

Shielding

Shielding is a kind of specific dribbling in which the player holds the ball away from an opponent while attempting to pass or dribble to a more desirable location. Teaching shielding helps less physical players get more comfortable with body contact. The technical aspect is side-on and arms out for creating distance between the ball and the defender. Side-on also provides a much stronger base of support than turning one's back to the opponent. Side-on also provides greater vision of teammates and opponents, thus offering more options.

A good activity for developing shielding skills is pairs working in a small 4 yard grid. Set up one grid for all to see. Start by using 'quick draw', which is two players facing each other, both with a foot on the ball and on coach's signal each tries to win the ball. Whoever wins the ball must shield the ball while remaining in the grid. Players should not kick the ball out of the grid. They attempt to win the ball and become the player shielding the ball in order to score a point. About every 10 seconds the coach calls out "Winner", and whoever has the ball at that time gets a point. If no one is shielding the ball at the coach's "Winner" signal, no one scores a point.

The main point of emphasis is that players often attempt too much dribbling (movement of the ball) instead of having their foot on the ball and using their body to keep the defender away from the ball. Usually one player or two will do this well so have them demonstrate to the others. Play 5 rounds and then switch partners, winners against winners.

The shielding player is doing a good job, but might not be quick enough for this aggressive defender.

Another shielding activity facilitating body contact is three players holding hands in a circular fashion with a ball in the middle and a fourth player on the outside attempting to get the ball. Forty second intervals are about right and then have a new player be on the outside. If the outside player wins the ball she simply returns it to the three circular players who were shielding. The player who won the ball the most times during her 40 second interval is the winner. Having players be in rigorous contact in game related situations is the correct way to teach assertive body contact as opposed to unsportsmanlike tactics that have no place in the game. Arms out is the correct way to make space for oneself. Throwing elbows is unsportsmanlike and can cause serious injury. It is also a violation of the game, causing possession to go to the opponents.

I think the smiles on all their faces says it all. Not only are they having fun but they're learning how to shield the ball and get accustomed to the contact that is an integral part of the game. I can't remember how many dozens of times coaches have asked me, "How do I make my players more aggressive?" My answer is, "We want strong assertion", and this is one of the activities I show to help them teach assertive play in a sportsmanlike manner.

Release the Prisoner

Two teams, everyone is dribbling in a 20 yard square grid. If a player's ball is kicked out of the grid by the opposing team, the player stands with legs apart (is a prisoner) and can be released to play again by a teammate passing a ball through her legs. Then that player can go get her ball and play again. The team with the least number of "prisoners" after 2 minutes wins.

Cross over the Bridge

Cross over the Bridge, sometimes called Lions and Rabbits, simply has players dribbling from one end of the grid to the other. A grid 15 x 25 yards is about right. The lion is in the center of the grid. All players have a ball and try to get past the Lion (start with the coach as the lion) and go to the opposite side of the grid. Anyone whose ball was hit becomes a lion. Play until there are only 2 or 3 players left, then restart the game. Growling and animation is encouraged.

A shortsided game that demands the player touch the ball five times before passing or shooting will help to perfect dribbling in a game environment. As players gain some success with this activity, confidence with the ball blossoms. Naturally, as players progress to passing/receiving stages, generally starting at about eight years of age, but seriously at twelve or more years old, one, two and three touch activities take a more prominent role.

One touch is clearly speed of play, used under heavy defensive pressure when receiving a properly paced ball, for layoffs or to get a ball forward as rapidly as possible to an open receiver. Two touches emphasize control and then an accurate pass or shot, often requiring power due to a distance situation. Three touches is an attempt to condition players to control the ball, 'blow by' an opponent and then make an accurate pass or shot.

The demand for one touch exercises at too early an age can cause bad habits because if no pass is available players just kick the ball mindlessly. More astute one touch possession exercises for speed of play often allow any number of touches, but the team that makes the first ten one touch passes is awarded a point. This allows for mindful possession and at the same time fosters speed of play.

Expert coaches, especially those highly experienced and licensed for youth coaching know that the abundance of dribbling and feinting moves accomplishes ball control, particularly when using all surfaces of the foot.

Eventually the player probably only uses two or three moves often, but if they are effective, players can go in either direction with a given move.

The most obvious, and probably the most important activity is to place the move introduced in a given session into a smallsided restricted game. Example: Let's say the Cruyff move of pulling the ball behind the standing foot was the focus of the dribbling warm-up and emphasis of the day's instruction. Therefore in the game every player must do a Cruyff move before passing. To facilitate success consider having defenders place hands on their head to allow players to make the Cruyff move. If that is insufficient have defenders stay two arm lengths away from the player with the ball until the move is made. Move to the team must make two Cruyff moves before going to goal. Move to unrestricted play and hope you see a couple of Cruyff moves used in appropriate situations.

For the very young another option is to have a single defender against the whole team so players can practice the move with minimal pressure.

By actually counting the number of touches when every player has a ball, in 10 minutes I found that youngsters average about 300 touches. Hard workers were in the 400 range. In any case almost all players will likely get over 450 touches in 15 minutes. This will ensure reaching the 800+ touches in a training session, which is the minimum number of touches desired for any youth training session. It is important to realize that lines, talking, and running without the ball all take away learning from the child's training session. In addition, motivation is reduced when no ball is being used.

JUGGLING

Much juggling can begin with self service hand tosses to very low heights of about 3 feet. Less of a toss may not be easier as one will not have adequate time to respond to the ball. Six feet or more presents a fear upon impact and a control problem for beginners. Multiple touches of air juggling are generally not productive for the youngest players because the ball being out of control for much of the time denies repetition. Juggling continuously with a single bounce allows much more successful repetition.

No-bounce juggling can start by having players do one juggle and catch the ball. First the thigh, which is easier, and move to using the foot. Try to get players to not have a lot of spin on the ball, which is accomplished by locking the ankle to a down position. Sometimes this single juggle with the ankle locked down is done in a sitting position. While standing move to two juggles. Move to two juggles with a single juggle with each foot and catch. Once players reach the stage where the vast majority can air juggle 5 or more times, move to pairs juggling. After this it is time to emphasize low to high body parts and high to low body parts juggling which is very game related. Another stage can be to juggle in groups of three, emphasizing control and pass (two touch) with a change of direction.

If you decide to have players keep at home records of juggling you must constantly remind them you have no interest in comparing one player to another, your sole interest is that each individual extend his/her own personal best! Clearly there could be many more steps in the juggling progression, or using a different order than recommended here, but juggling is an important ball control skill. Of special importance is the game related high to low control, use of heading in the juggling and the changes of direction juggling skill.

Many programs offer patches for certain levels of juggling achievements. This often encourages players to practice on their own.

Recording the number of juggles at home helps to get honest responses and helps the youngster to focus on his personal improvement instead of being concerned with the accomplishments of other players.

Juggling and heading progressions are never done for an entire training session. Instead the coach attempts to get 5 to 10 minutes of juggling at successive sessions. Often even mature teams spend a few minutes on these technical skills as part of their warm-up.

Here the players are being given some time for juggling during practice. At the same time the coach is encouraging players to juggle on their own. Keeping a record of their highest number of juggles from home sometimes helps to get them to touch the ball on their own.

Juggling in threes is best to encourage two touches. That's game related.
Control the ball on the first touch, pass or shoot with the second touch.

Three's is ideal for learning to turn the ball with the head and other body parts, and also creates the incentive to work hard. Of course learning to make a good decision quickly as to which body part to use is another benefit.

PASSING/RECEIVING, COLLECTION

These two topics are so intertwined that it makes sense to combine them. One might better express the domain by calling it receiving/passing because this is the general true order of this skill.

Moving from the dribbling stage to the passing/receiving stage is a sensitive area of development. Sensitive because we do not want to undo all the hard work of developing a youngster's confidence of ball control and dribbling skills. In many cases this is exactly what happens because one of the most important elements to win games depends upon passing quality. In a typical situation parents, and unfortunately many coaches, begin to call out "Boot it!" or similar phrases such as "Kick it!", "Pass it!" or "Send it!". This can lead to meaningless kicking of the ball to no particular receiver or location.

Fortunately there are methods to move from dribbling to passing/receiving in a constructive way so as to develop team play. Unfortunately these methods are known by a miniscule number of youth experts. Several of these methods of advancing further development as opposed to confusing or destroying the hard work of developing the competent dribbler follow. These methods incorporate combination play so that instead of thwarting development, players are raised to an even higher level.

Again the activity environment, in this case the design of shortsided games, teaches what we want the players to learn.

Divided Field Four Goal Game

This is an activity designed to have players change the point of attack with no accompanying instruction. Here the added dimension of raising the level of the quality dribbler is added, as opposed to discouraging his talent and accomplishments.

Players cannot dribble across the cone divided field area; instead the ball must be passed across the cone dividing line. On the first occasion of this activity there is a single cone dividing line. After several sessions a second dividing line can be added horizontally with the same inducement of passing the ball over the line as opposed to dribbling over the 'line'. Pugg goals or other small goals are ideal for this activity. If necessary flag poles or cones will do. The approximate field size is 35 yards wide and 25 yards long. The width being greater than the length fosters the change in point of attack without an abundance of coaching.

In this game the accomplished dribbler can get the ball back by passing, and then receiving a return wall pass, thus developing combination play and passing/moving skills, both of which are vital steps to higher level soccer! Thus instead of ruining the hard work of establishing dribbling and ball control, the player is raised to the level of combination play and mobility!

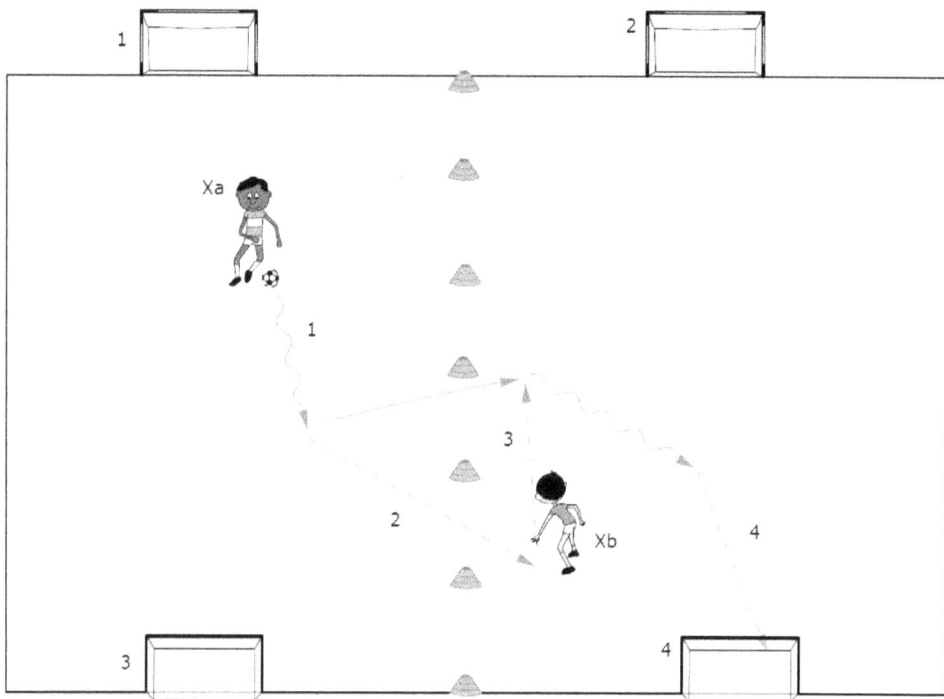

#1 Xa wins the ball and dribbles toward his goals; we assume defenders are blocking Xa's ability to go straight forward and score on goal 3; #2 so Xa passes to Xb and runs across the cone line;
 #3 Xb returns the ball one touch to Xa; #4 Xa receives and scores a goal.
Thus instead of having the other players merely watch the accomplished dribbler, combination play is developed and all members of the team move to higher levels of soccer understanding.

If the coach chooses an even greater form of inducement, award one point every time the ball is passed over a dividing line.

Option: No shots on goal until two passes are made.

Option: Using two lines, a vertical and a horizontal cone line, in a possession game requires the ball be passed across both lines, awarding a point every time this occurs. Goals count 3 points. The team that gets 8 points first wins. Play the best of 3 rounds. The possible wrinkles for this basic activity are innumerable. Try your own.

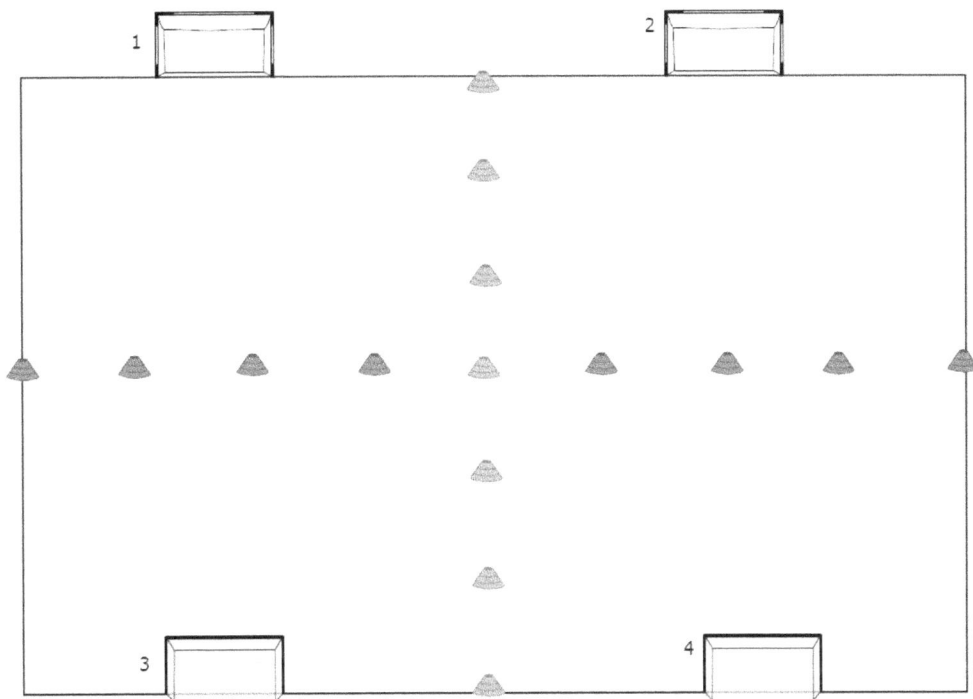

Players must pass the ball over both the field divided cone lines.

The following four goal activity, not the combination play clarified in the previous paragraphs, generally causes players with advanced instincts to go to the far goal and another player with able vision will pass him the ball. Be patient and wait for it to happen and then offer praise and a demonstration of this advanced tactic (changing the point of attack) by your youngsters.

While it is easy to say "Why wasn't one of the defenders marking O4?", pressure and cover on the ball is not only common, it is even correct. Probably X4 would have been more properly positioned had she been somewhere in line with the long pass that was made, yet even in the professional game players on the opposite side of the field (away from the ball) are hardly ever marked. In the case of professionals, there are not two goals at the end of the field and so the strategy is not as much of a problem.

Here the four goal game is using flags and it looks like the coach found his keeper/sweeper and his midfield defender (ball winner).

It looks like one of our young ladies is tactically way ahead of her age level, and better still her teammate saw her and passed the ball to her. She even scored the goal!

Also see the flat-faced goal activity in the support chapter, which also aids change in point of attack. Actually there are many activities throughout the text that encourage receiving/passing without prohibiting dribbling.

Pairs facing Each other

While not competitive, this offers so many repetitions in a very short time that it can be used in the warm-up for brief periods of time to benefit player technique.

Here the coach is refining all the technical details of the push pass using pairs facing each other. Note the coach is in a position to see all the players and make individual suggestions, corrections or maybe ask a question to get the players to take more ownership of their efforts.

Simply have pairs facing each other, one partner on a line of the field and all the groups side by side about 7 yards apart so the coach can see and work with all the players.

Put two of the most competent players as the middle group so all can easily see them when you use those players for demonstration purposes. When the coach does the demonstration use a very long exaggerated follow through. The one difference between passing and receiving with the inside of the foot is the leg is pulled backward for receiving and follows through forward when passing.

In any case the collection with the feet is started with using the inside of the foot positioning to receive the ball with three surfaces: inside frontal area of the heel, just below the inside of protruding ankle bone, and rear inside area of the big toe area.

H.A.T.

The acronym "HAT" heel, ankle, toe might help your players. In any case it will allow a quick, efficient reminder. By using this broad surface area, ball control reception is maximized.

This player has her toe up and it appears that she is going to strike the ball using all three of the correct areas of contact for the push pass.

The major points of this important basic skill are:
- Move to the ball when receiving. After receiving move backward to create space. In Basics of Basics the emphasis was on moving to the ball; in this exercise both using space and making space is demanded. Move to the ball, move away after the pass.
- Use one foot to collect and the other to pass to your partner (right/left or left/right); this causes much faster play for ALL AGE LEVELS
- See the ball onto your foot
- Make eye contact with receiver before passing the ball
- Receive and pass the ball with the exact same surface ("HAT")
- In collecting move the ball at about a 45° angle in the direction of the foot which you are going to strike the ball with; a distance of about 4 feet is a reasonable guideline; discourage trapping a ball dead as it slows down play, forcing the head down and reducing vision
- Toes locked upward; the opposite position of when doing a power instep drive
- Non-kicking foot pointed to location of the pass
- Look at the target location, but see the ball when you strike it!
- Long leg swing, long stroke, with huge follow through; no chopping at the ball

Generally the biggest problem is not turning the foot (ankle), knee and hip adequately so the ball can hit the three surfaces. It may take five or more such sessions before a great deal of the above coaching skill points become ingrained into the players' behavior. Keep on moving among the group giving individual attention, complimenting as well as correcting.

At a later stage, age 10 to 12, the same format can be used for outside the foot receiving/passing, turns, air chest collection, chipping, Cruyff collection, dummy pass to self, speed dribble-away and turn, and other more advanced skills. Well after the inside of foot ball control is established, instruct advanced receiving FRONT FOOT collection and passing when the opponent is behind the receiver. This creates distance away from an opponent and is more deceptive.

Passing and Shooting Warm Up

This is a competitive game with a 3 yard wide cone gate goal set up between the two opposing sides of 2v2. A flat disc or vest is placed at both sides about 8 yards from the gate goal. The hard return kick to opponents must be taken from behind the vest/cone. This is a continuous motion exercise. Whenever scored upon start again with friendly service.

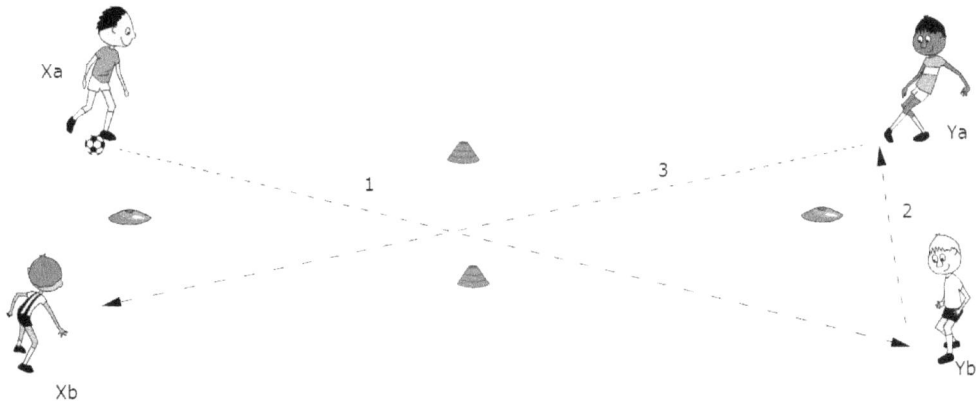

#1 Xa to start is giving friendly service through the cone goal to the Y team, in this case Yb. Friendly groundball moderately paced speed is a demand for starting the game. #2 Yb serves an excellent one touch pass to teammate Ya. #3 Ya will send the ball through the cone goal at a fast pace to the opponents with the hope they cannot return it two touch. Whenever opponents cannot return the ball with both players having played one touch, a point is scored.

Service must be friendly; if unfriendly and the coach observes it, take away a point from that team.

One option is to pair a weak player with a strong player on each team in hopes that the weak player will learn by observing and copying the strong player. This also helps to balance the teams. With some encouragement from the coach, maybe more advanced players will help the weaker players to improve. Players coaching each other greatly enhances team development.

A 'Group of the Whole' is a very useful format for many skills, but is outstanding for receiving/passing in a somewhat realistic environment. All players are in a group, in this case about one ball for every three players. Players simply dribble and pass to one another. This is also good for increasing communication, vision and even serves as a bit of team building. Be certain all players circulate around the whole area and that no little subgroups form. At a much later stage for more reality have a single defender moving around to kick balls away. Another wrinkle is to have two teams with different colored vests and you can only pass to members of your team. Another wrinkle is you can only pass to the opposite team. One, two, three touch demands are all excellent. Extended dribbling with changes of speed and direction could be an eight touch dribbling option. It really is a very versatile environment that can be used for dozens of activities. It provides many touches of the ball. Be certain that no matter what your activity, all players keep moving and communicating.

Once players have been taught the power instep kick, use a large area and demand long passes. Be certain to remind players not to hit an intervening unsuspecting teammate with the ball. A 'Group of the Whole' is excellent for wall passes, takeovers, overlaps and many other skills. Certainly double passes, skip passes, alternating controlled dribbling with a one touch pass are all possibilities. For players above age twelve, flicks, chips, bent balls and other advanced skills come into play. The advantage of a 'Group of the Whole' is that it entails much visual development, thinking in the form of decision making of where to go in addition to being a good basic team building format.

It normally will take many reminders to get the team to use the whole area! Players will not learn to use the whole field on offense in games if it is not demanded consistently in all training activities.

This simply is the whole team in warm-up following the coaches commands. In this instance, usually the beginning phase, everyone has a ball. It appears that he has asked for toe taps. Generally evolves into competitive activities such as hit another players ball, exchange balls, musical chairs, etc. In this format a coach can nearly attain 200 plus touches for each player in 10 minutes!

Simply passing around a one yard cone goal or flag will provide very simple receiving/passing skill development. This can be done all the way down to age 6.

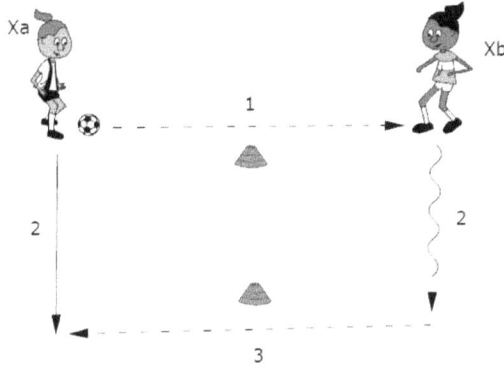

#1 Xa passes to Xb, #2 Xb dribbles across the face of the cone goal while Xa is moving across to receive the return pass #3 Xb passes back to Xa and the exercise continues.

This environment has dozens of wrinkles such as having hand air ball service, heading, two touch, feints, dribbling moves and innumerable other possibilities. The one touch option usually starts with both players passing directly to each other through the inside of the gate goal. For two touch options encourage the use of both feet throughout the entire exercise.

2 V 1 to Goal

A way to have meaningful passing/receiving is to have pairs attack a goal against a single defender. All groups should be working simultaneously. If necessary, have some working toward a regular goal while others work toward flags or cone goals. Pugg goals are excellent for this purpose. Be sure that if some are using cone goals and others regular goals that groups switch places so all feel they have had an equal opportunity. Two counter attack cone goals should be provided for the defender, if he wins the ball. Either a dribble through or passing through the cone goals can be required. A flat-faced goal can have two groups working on each side, thus accommodating 12 players.

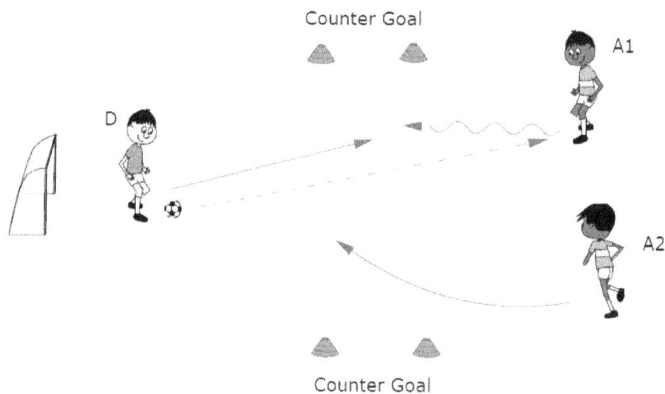

The attackers are about 20 yards from the goal. The defender serves a crisp ball to one of the attackers and then defends the goal. Attackers pass and dribble to score a goal. A1 went to the ball and then dribbled at Defender D.

Every four minutes, rotate a new defender. After three rounds the defender who gave up the least number of goals is the winner. This just simplifies the scoring, but since this is a 2v1 attacking topic no instruction is given to the defending aspect of the exercise. By not giving instruction to any of the players this becomes a discovery activity allowing players to figure out possibilities for themselves, thus promoting initiative and creativity. Naturally, if the exercise were used for defensive purposes, usually after the offensive roles are somewhat perfected, then the coaching points would be for the defenders.

3 v 1 Keep Away

Another simple passing/receiving activity is 3v1 with the defender in a triangle. The defender is changed by the coach every 3 minutes. Ages 9-12 should be able to switch the defender whenever the ball is won. The 5 and 6 year olds should do this exercise at least 3 times without a defender! Simply passing the ball to a teammate through the triangle may be an appropriate challenge in early stages of development.

Once players can receive and pass with a two touch demand, move to a crab defender, followed by hands behind the back defender and finally an unrestricted defender. Recall that age does not determine progression to higher level activity; ability is the determining factor. Be certain that players are within 5 yards of the triangle. A 6 yard triangle is about right. Reduce or enlarge to equalize success and challenge for the given level of your players.

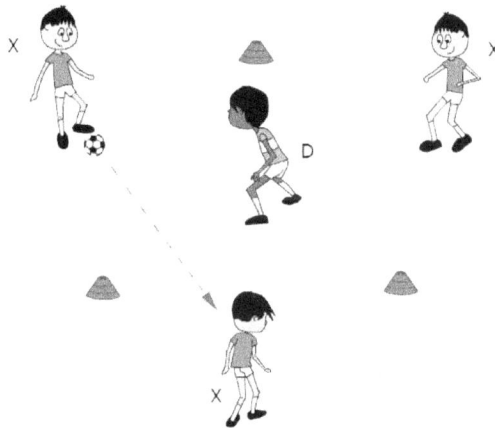

This exercise of passing/receiving with a defender demands feinting in order for the players to succeed. This can be mentioned and demonstrated by an able player or if the coach is capable she can demonstrate feinting a pass in one direction and then passing it in another. Head fakes, body movement accompanied by foot/leg movement are the most effective. At upper ages, once success in unrestricted touches is attained, move to two touches. In this and almost all exercises the ball should not be stationary for even two seconds.

This group was having good success with the 3v1 passing through the triangle exercise. Change the defender regularly. Be certain receiver's move to the support the ball.

Going to goal is the next stage. 3 v 1 to a goal is an adequate challenge for the very youngest age levels. The three can start about 30 yards from the goal and the defender can start from the goal line.

As always, follow with an actual game, possibly beginning with the inducement that X number of passes must be made before going to goal. Do not encourage long ball kicks to nowhere as is often complimented by parents during actual matches---especially if their child kicked the ball. Compliment good receptions and passes with clear intended receivers. End the session with unrestricted play, as this is what players experience on match days. If you never have players play unrestricted it is meaningless to expect good decisions during regular matches. Unrestricted play has nearly no coaching, but much observation for preparing future sessions. It is conducted so that players can experience the full enjoyment of the game. It also allows players to learn from their mistakes and good executions of their skill. Creativity is thwarted when all training sessions have instruction and restrictions for the entire session.

feinting Passing to create Time for Receiver

Four corner goals, 4 players, 2 balls as shown in diagram---in this case one ball at the bottom left and one at the top right. Simply start with the ball at opposing cones. The cone grid area is 15 yards square with the grid goals about 2 yards wide. There is no problem with odd numbers; simply place an extra player at any location.

Xc dribbles to the central area and feints a pass to Xa to her left, but passes to the right to Xd. Simultaneously Xb also with a ball dribbles to the central area, feints to her left and passes to Xa at her right. Note that Xc has sprinted to the Xb original location and Xb sprinted to the Xc original location. Now Xa and Xd have the balls so they repeat the process.

Be certain that the receivers stand well behind the cone goal and move to the ball. This facilitates the demand of the passer making an accurate pass through the gate. Demand eye contact for the feint as well as the pass to the receiver. Review the elements of the inside of the foot push pass, especially "HAT".

Players simply go straight ahead after the pass to get ready to be receivers. Both players going at the same time creates a token form of defense, forcing visual skills and timing adjustments.

The feint should actually have the player look AND move the leg in the feinting direction and then pass the other way. Generally the inside of the foot push pass to the right is made with the left foot. Be certain to spend some time going in the opposite direction; feinting right and passing to the left with the right foot.

It is nearly impossible to overstate the importance of early introduction of feinting skills, in this case in the passing situation. In the dribbling section the entire section was devoted to moves, all of which were feinting of an opponent.

This is a continuous motion exercise that accomplishes many repetitions in a short period of time. With eight or more players set up more than one group. With odd numbers simply place the extra player at any location and the first one in the line goes and the other goes on the next repetition.

At a much later stage of development, ages 11-20, the outside the foot laces pass can be employed, however the distances would be considerably greater.

Sequence Passing

This is nothing more than having groups of players number themselves 1 through 5 for five players, often played with 4 or even 3 player groups. 1 must pass to 2, 2 to 3 etc. and finally 5 passes to 1 and the sequence goes on continuously. Some of the common requirements are: 2 touch passing, 1 touch, or even 3 touch passing. Other possibilities are 1 must do a wall pass with 2, then with 3 all the way to number 5. Finally one gives the ball to #2 who does the same thing with 3 through 1. This same procedure could be done with takeovers and mini-overlaps, though overlaps will likely only succeed with age 11 or older. This could be done with each group in a separate area, but by about age 10 or 11 sequence passing can have all the groups in the same area sort of causing low level defensive pressure for each other. In this case the skills of controlling the ball, passing and getting the head up demands much more visual skill development.

At age 14 and above coaches sometimes play possession games with the demand of sequence passing. This is well beyond the scope of age groups covered in this text. With the 6-8 age group quality push passes could be the requirement. Ages 7-9 might emphasize a given type of turn. Do collection emphasis for ages 9-12 with the requirement of a long 15 to 20 yards instep kick pass. Actually sequence passing can accommodate many different skills, the setup is determined by the skill/tactic the coach wants to develop.

The coaching points of emphasis are: All players moving with and without the ball, players off the ball try to get to a visible location for the player who is going to pass to them. Sometimes the activity gets too crunched together and the coach must require passes be 10 plus yards or whatever he deems most appropriate. When players make a good effort this activity fosters anticipation skills very well. All coaches recognize this as a very important skill that is not easily taught.

Passing Grid

There are literally hundreds of passing patterns. This is one of the simplest passing grids for the very young players. 12 x 12 yards will suffice. For older groups increase the size. X1 passes to X2 and runs forward to X2's position. The process simply continues around the grid. Note that there are 5 players, as the first location requires two players so there is someone there when X4 gets to pass to the starting location. Strongly encourage two touches, one to receive and one to pass the ball to the next location. For 10 or more players, definitely have two groups.

Be certain players do not use up all the space with dribbling between them and the receiver. This ruins the exercise, but more importantly is a bad habit for actual game playing because it allows easy double teaming by the opponents.

Passing Grid with Layoff Service

Strongly encourages eye contact, learning the correct distance to lead a receiver and also one touch control.

#1 Xb checks to Xa, Xa passes to Xb; #2 Xb lays the ball off to Xa; #3 Xb spins around the cone and receives a lead pass from Xa; #4 Xb passes to Xc and the cycle continues with each player moving forward after they pass the ball. Repetition sequence is pass to feet, layoff, lead pass.

Geared more to ages 8-12 or players with at least two or three years of soccer experience. There are dozens of these passing pattern grids all with different valuable purposes. This is a good exercise to introduce the spin out and the layoff, which simply means that Xb turns away from the cone to receive the lead pass from Xa.

Double Pass Grid Passing

After your pass across the grid cones follow your pass (original positions Xa & Xc). If in the double pass location (left and right wide spots) follow your pass after the double pass.

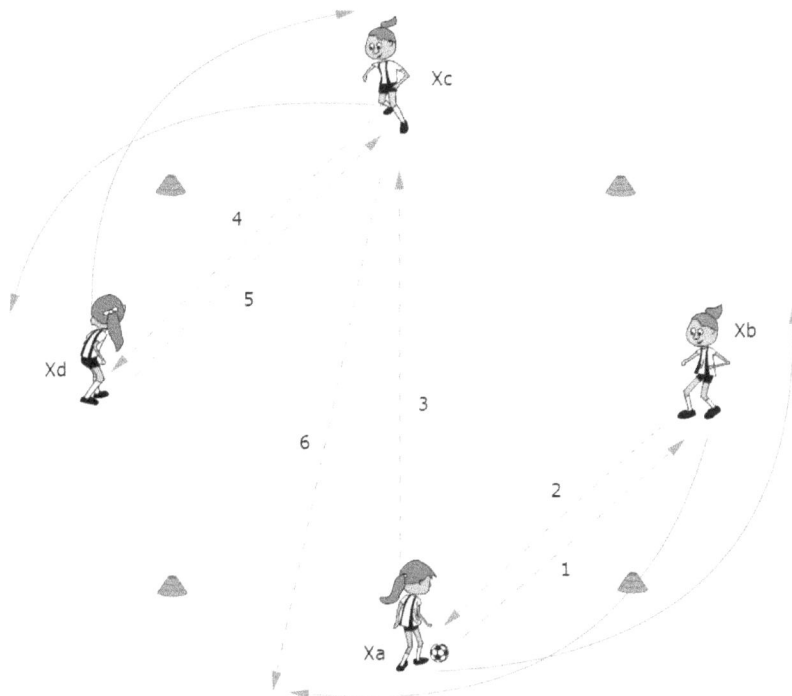

The grid cones are 12 x 12 yards.
#1 Xa has the ball and passes to Xb; #2 Xb returns the ball to Xa and follows her pass; #3 Xa then passes across the grid to Xc and runs behind the Xb location; #4 Xc passes to Xd; #5 Xd returns it to Xc and follows the pass #6 Xc passes to Xb and runs behind the Xd location; #7 Xb passes to Xa since everyone followed their pass; Then the process simply continues. The pattern is double pass, straight across the grid, double pass, straight across the grid continuously.

No matter how simple the pattern, it takes some time to teach. Clearly more for ages 9-12. No one would ever do a given pattern exercise unless they intended to use it more than once, due to the time necessary for establishing the pattern. Focus is on quality passing/receiving, eye contact, going to the ball and movement. Have youngsters stand back from the grid so they can move toward the passes as required in Basics of Basics. After competency has been established two groups can compete to see who can make 40 passes first! Have players count aloud for quality administration/organization.

Wall Passing Grid

About 15 x 15 yard grids: Use 2 or 3 grids according to number of players present. Players Pa to Ph are placed as shown.

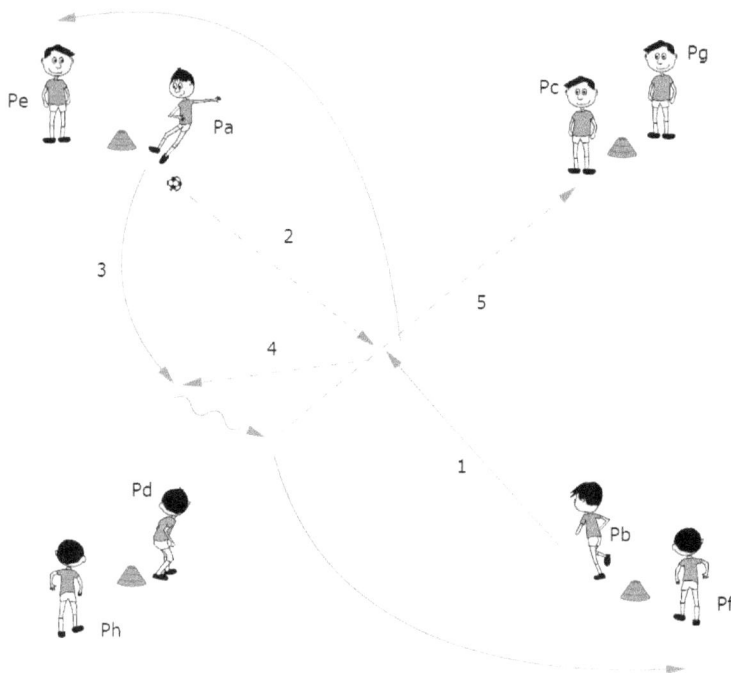

#1 Pa has the ball, Pb shows hard by running toward Pa; #2 Pa passes to Pb; #3 Pa runs for the return wall pass; #4 Pb delivers the wall pass one touch; #5 Pa passes to Pc; and the process continues with Pd showing for the ball from Pc. Showing means moving to where you want the ball.

Everyone simply follows his or her pass. Generally there are 2 players in each corner of the grid.

Demand accurate passes. For young players that means inside of the foot push passes, eye contact, showing for the ball. The pass is the FIRST STEP OF ACCELERATION TO RECEIVE THE RETURN PASS. Geared to ages 10-12. Very talented younger groups are a possibility.

Coaching Points: Side on facing teammates; accelerate with pass-touch; eye contact communication; see the ball when striking it; bent runs; quality passes---top spin achieved by striking the ball just above the vertical center; knee over ball; see moving players location; communication; insure wall passer uses one touch; cover up for teammates mistakes!

Double Grid Crease Passing

Double Grid Crease Passing simply has two groups passing in two grids separated by about 5 yards.

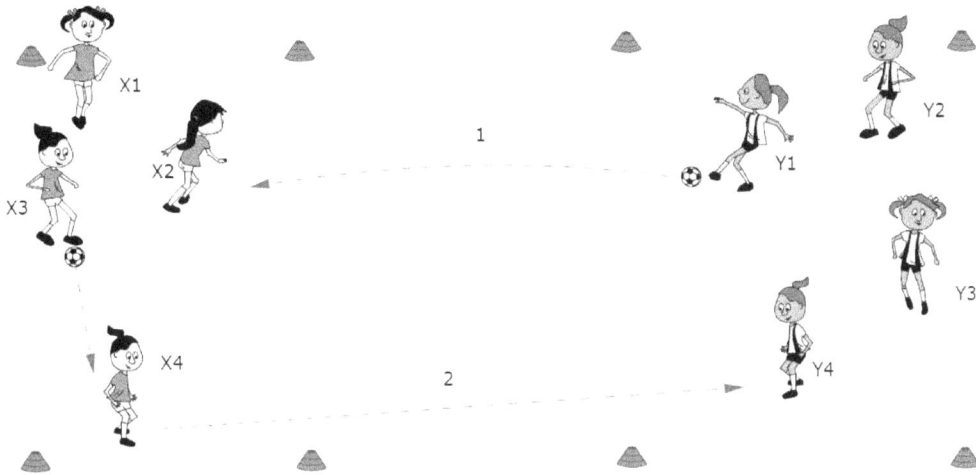

One ball in each grid and after 5 passes one of the groups passes to an open player in the opposite grid. Eye contact, possibly verbal communication is used to insure completion.

#1 in this case Y1 passes to X2 and X4 just received a pass from X3 and so she passed the ball to Y4. Play simply continues in this fashion. The goal is to have one ball in each grid all the time.

Options for **subsequent** sessions:
Progression 1 for mature groups: add one or two defenders in the area between the two grids.
Progression 2 has a defender in each area as the groups are passing.
Progression 3 encourage takeovers, heel passes and wall passes.
Progression 4 the pass to the opposite grid must be a one touch pass
Progression 5 is requiring one touch pass when the ball is received from the other grid.

This exercise is also excellent for vision training. Simply have teams play possession using a large grid area. Every consecutive 5 passes is a point.

Scrimmage: Move to going to goals with the requirement of 5 passes before a shot. Generally the best passing/receiving team wins most of the time. For this reason, good coaches spend a great deal of time in passing/receiving possession exercises.

1v1 GAMES

1v1 is obviously a foundational skill to the whole game of soccer. Some would say the team that wins the most 1v1 battles wins the game. Maybe. Many would say the team that passes and receives the best, which generally depends upon good support, would win the game. First of all this text is about developing players, but certainly the team with the best players, good 1v1 ability, good receiving/passing and good support skills will be at an enormous advantage. Certainly much of the game depends upon 1v1 ability. What follows is over a dozen 1v1 formats that involve young players in experiencing dribbling, ball contact, competition and fun. 1v1 formats number in the hundreds.

Simple 1v1 using two cone goals will place dribbling in an easy competitive fun format.

Xa is with the ball trying to score on the right side cone goals. If Ya wins the ball he simply tries to score at the goal on the left. After 1 minute the two b players play 1v1.

Two pairs can work on the same setup, causing some necessity for use of visual skills. In this manner 3 setups can accommodate 12 players. Using a big area all 6 pairs could work on 2 Pugg Goals about 20+ yards apart. Switch partners every 4 minutes. Winners against winners.
Option: 1v1 difficulty can be increased by simply using a single large cone at each end as the goal.

For even greater difficulty have a single cone goal for both players. 1v1 is very rigorous so water breaks and brief coaching points provide the rests needed to maintain a quality effort. Also, change partners often and provide a one minute break between games.

4 Goals

Another format that helps increase the success of the 1v1 and at the same time greatly encourages changes of direction is a set up as shown. Actual goals for the attacker and cone or flag goals for the defender will suffice.

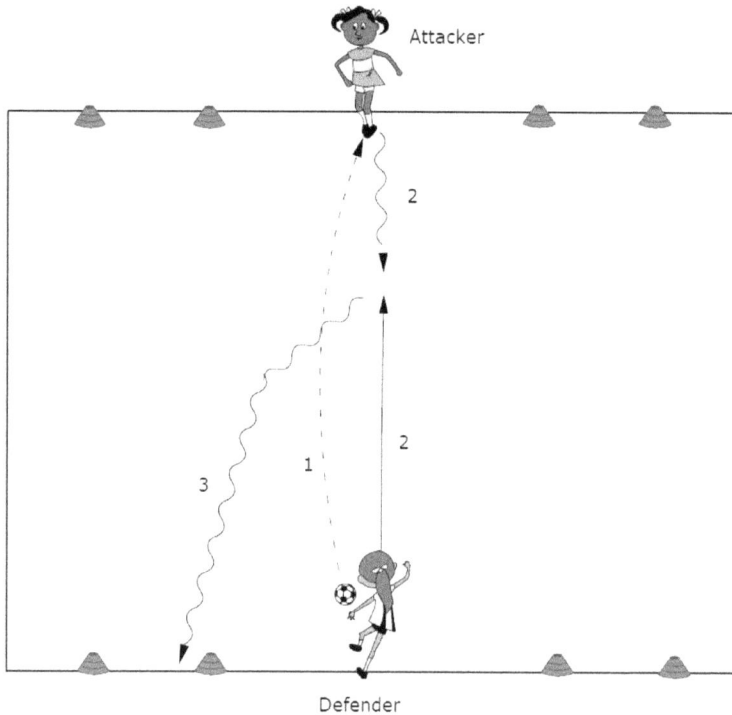

#1 the defender (D) serves a ball to the attacker; #2 attacker dribbles the ball toward the two goals at the bottom of the grid while the defender runs to close down space and tries to defend the two bottom goals or win the ball from the attacker. #3 attacker beat defender and scored a goal. If the defender wins the ball she tries to score on one of the two upper counter goals.

Again this setup can accommodate 2 or 3 pairs with some at times working in the opposite direction! Often in these exercises have the requirement to dribble through, instead of merely passing the ball through the goal. If using the dribbling requirement that simply means that the first touch of the ball after it goes through the cone goal is made by the offensive player in order to score a point. Generally by putting their foot on the ball. Players switch roles after each trial. Every 4 to 6 players should have their own setup.

The most important aspect of 1v1 is that players get many trials. Remember, the ball and the game are the most important teachers! Change partners regularly.

Triangle Goal

Triangle Goal is another simple 1v1 format that is tons of fun. Simply have 3 cones or obstacle poles as shown. Generally 6 yards apart is about right. Up to 5 or 6 pairs can work on the same setup.

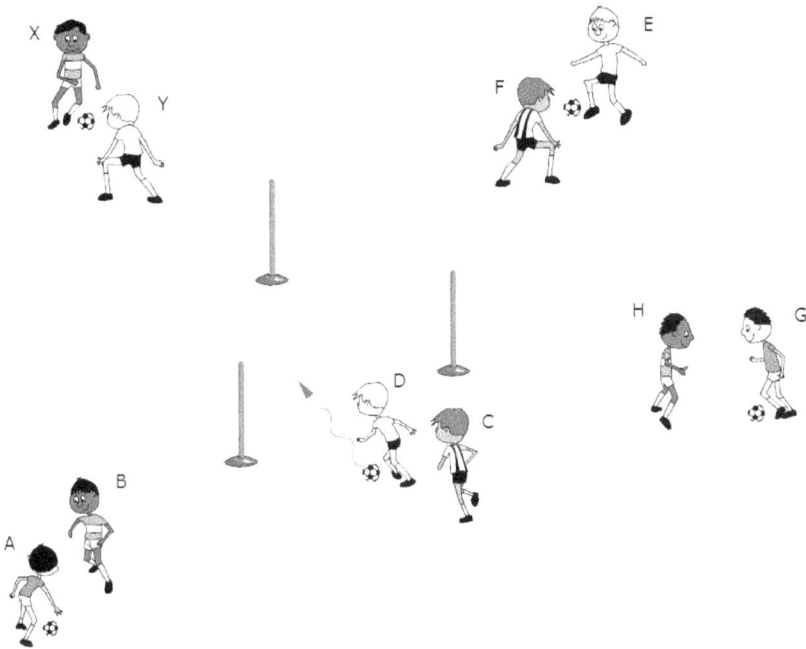

Players can score on the triangular goal from any direction. The requirement is that you must dribble into the goal. The scorer maintains possession, leaves the triangle goal area from where he entered and tries to score again from a different entry than the one he scored on. D has just beat C and has scored. Defenders must win the ball to become attackers. The player with the most goals in 3 minutes wins.

Two of my pairs wandered off the grid, but the two visible pairs seem to be working very hard.

Pairs should be evenly matched for this activity or else a weak player will be discouraged by a skillful player, and at the same time there is no instructional challenge (fun) for the strong player. If this is not possible, simply change partners after short intervals of 3 to 4 minutes.

This format is excellent for 2v2, 3v3 or even for a whole team, which at early ages probably means 4 or 5 aside.

1 v 1 to Full Size Goals with Keepers

1v1 to Full Size Goals with Keepers: Game starts with a defender serving to the attacker. Goals are 30 yards apart and the width about 24 yards with up to 4 pairs working simultaneously. If there are more than 4 pairs one half would be working the 1v1 to the goals and the others would juggle or do station exercises. Turn this into a tournament and you have a complete exciting practice. Warm-up of 15 minutes and then winners against winners, two 5 minute halves with 2 minutes rest at half time.

You can see clearly how this is extremely game related, provides abundant repetition and thus causes much player development.

outside Neutrals I v I

Grid is 10 by 20 yards. This involves the wall pass. It also embodies pass and move and to some extent getting the head up for increased vision. Feinting remains prominent, passing as well as timing all come into play. Here there simply are two cones or obstacle course marker goals about 8 yards wide, and neutrals one on each side of the grid as shown in the diagram. Neutral players are used for the wall pass. Wall passes are sometimes referred to as 'give and goes' or 1-2's.

This is a feinting wall pass emphasis exercise; therefore the feint is required on every trial. #1 Dribbling X has just faked a pass to N1 #2 then passed to N2 and ran behind Y (blind side run); #3 then received the one touch pass from N2; #4 X scored a goal. This is a directional activity with each player having to attack a specific goal. When Y wins the ball he simply attacks the left side goal. Goals are one point, but goals employing a wall pass count 3 points. Double passes are permitted, but do not score any points.

1v1 is very rigorous, therefore neutrals switch in every 3 minutes.

Multiple Goals in a Line

This next 1v1 exercise puts a high premium on feinting as it is nearly impossible to score without quality feinting in this setup. Simply place a line of cones about 5 yards apart and one of the pair defends a particular goal as a line defender. Line defender means the player can only move left and right along the imaginary goal line.

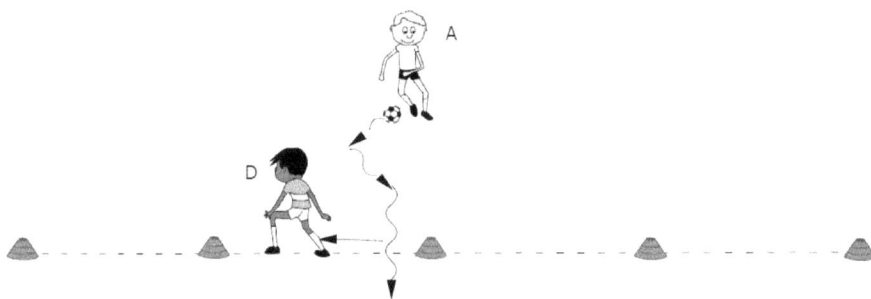

If the player scores he simply attacks his partner going in the opposite direction. If the defender wins the ball he becomes the attacker.

This is a very rigorous activity which requires breaks. Certainly one break can be a water break. Switch pairs every 3 minutes, winners against winners. It could even be a mini-tournament if you so desire. Compliment creativity such as a player double feinting, crossing the line and only going a yard or two over the line and immediately crossing the line again in the opposite direction. This also puts the defender on his toes and introduces the rudiments of fast defensive recovery.

6 Goals Reduced to 2 Goals

David Goodman of Connecticut has promoted this next activity that allows a single setup to be used for the entire training session by simply making minor adjustments. The setup is 6 cone goals arranged as diagrammed. Goals are 2 yards wide, about 10 yards apart width wise and about 20 yards distant from each other.

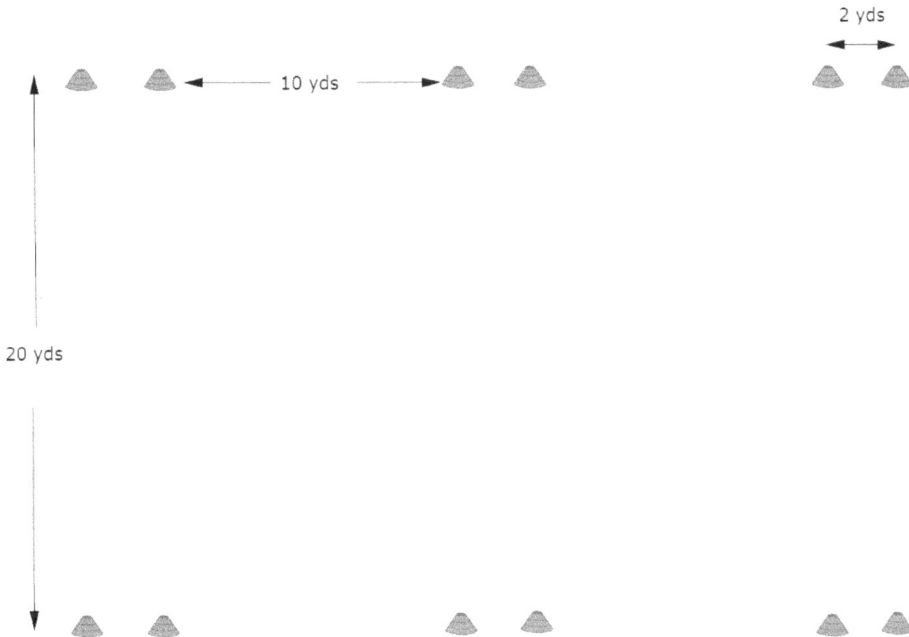

The first stage is 1v1 to any goal in direction the attacker is going. To start, the player begins from his defending goal.

Second stage is 1v1 to one particular goal.

Third stage is 2v2 to any goal, then to a particular goal.

Move to 3v3, probably to a single pair of goals. With 12 it would be one group on each of the outside pairs of goals.

Finally move to using all players; then simply use the central pair of goals, lengthen the field and remove the inside cones of the outside goals, leaving the four corner cones to define the playing area. Do not allow anyone to be a goalkeeper. If you desire goalkeepers make the goal much larger. Just include a simple warm-up of a group of the whole and you have an excellent complete training session!

1 v 1 with Full Size Goals for Age Level

Note players are not right next to the goal posts. This is a safety factor that should be required for all activities.

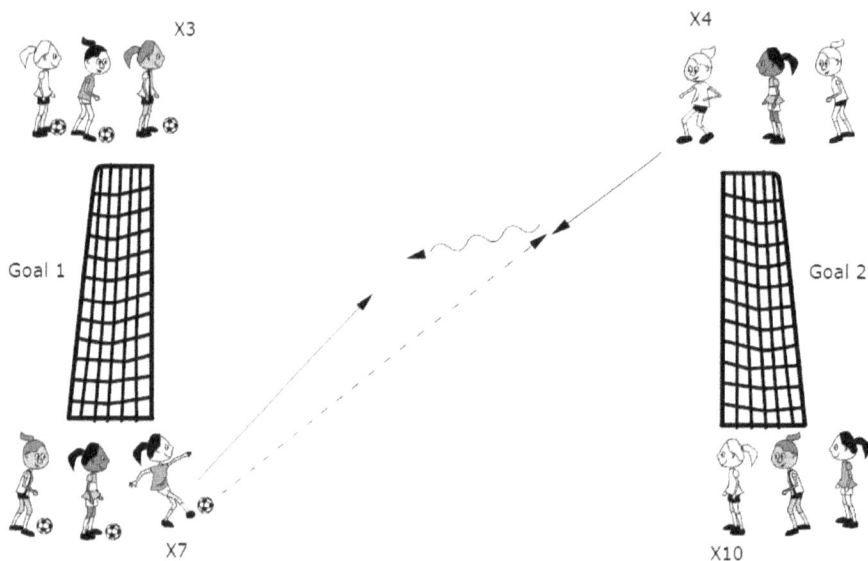

X7 sends a crisp driven ball to X4 and runs to defend while X4 attempts to score on goal 1.

Note all players on the left have a ball for serving. The next service is X3 to X10, and so forth. Player rotation is clockwise. Players retrieve all shots not on goal and do so with pace as demanded by the coach. Demand rapid service even to the point that the server anticipates the previous group's shot. Distance can be from 20 to 35 yards depending on the ability level of players.

Either a time limit or number of touches limit is generally incorporated into this activity, as an enormous number of touches are totally unrealistic in game situations. Somewhere between 5 and 10 touches would be reasonable or else it would be nothing more than creating a bad habit when going to goal.

Coaching Points: The defender runs at high speed immediately after service. In fact, the service pass is the first speed step taken! Once the defender gets near the attacker he assumes a low, knees bent, legs shoulder width apart, arms out, boxer stance with one leg in front of the other, and EYES ON THE BALL. The last steps are small steps. The attacker attempts to blow by the defender with a move, change of direction and change of speed.

The first time or two it is best to not have keepers. After having done this activity several times, add a keeper, with emphasis on the attacker looking to shoot to the open area of the goal.

If the defender wins the ball he attacks the goal on the right, in which case service is immediate, so two groups are working at opposite directions at the same time. Actually two groups can always work at the same time.

Generally, stoppages are only for correction of items that pertain to nearly the whole team, but individualized correction is emphasized throughout. The sandwich approach is best. This approach is positive opening/correction/ positive close (how this will make you a better player). Example: "Marie, you got there early for the tackle, but you have to be lower, this will help you win the tackle." In early stages always emphasize attack, because without a reasonable attack the defense requires little effort and is therefore fruitless.

Goal Line Numbers

Two teams with players numbered 1 through however many players there are on each team. The coach is on the goal line about 2 yards from the goal. Players are all about 5 yards away from the goal post, also on the goal line. The coach calls out a number and those players, one from each team, play 1v1 for the ball that the coach has sent out about 15 yards from the goal line (distance depends upon ability level). The first round can simply be #1 followed by #2 etc. but after that, call out the numbers at random to maintain focus. After about 5 rounds of 1v1, move to calling out two numbers so now we have 2v2 situations. Eventually move to 3v3, followed by a couple of rounds of all the players. With the whole team option the ball is usually sent out about 30 yards. Move to traditional scrimmage using two teams and two goals. Three points for a goal and one point for every time a player beats someone in a 1v1 situation.

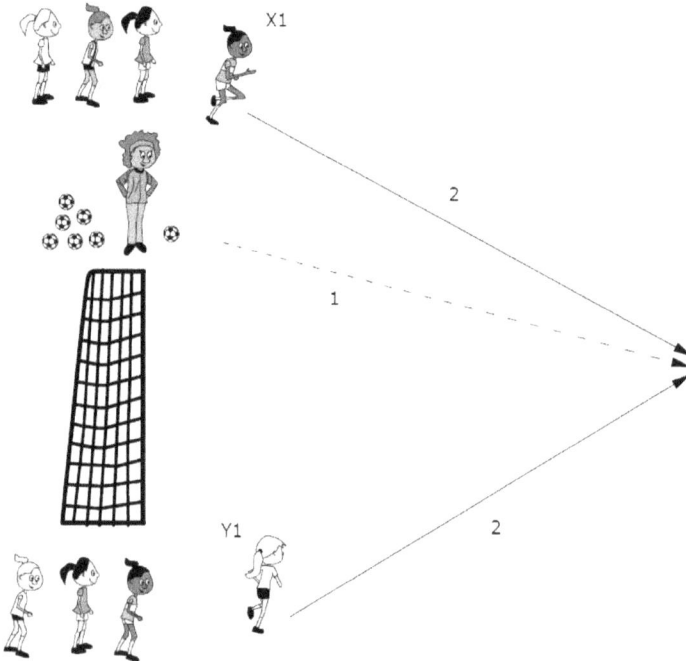

#1 the coach sent out a neutral service ball for X1 and Y1 to compete for: #2 whoever wins the ball attacks the goal and the other defends. Players keep team score. Players need to learn to be the score keepers so the coach can focus on coaching instead of being a score keeper. Attempt to match player numbers to ability.

Spots

Five "spots" marked with cones in relation to a goal. This setup will serve 10 players. At first no keeper is used. In subsequent sessions add a keeper. Unfortunately, game repetitions are reduced considerably with a keeper since only one pair at a time can go in order to protect the keeper. If two goals are available you may be able to only have 3 stations on each goal, allowing the number of repetitions to be much greater which increases the fun, fitness and development of 1v1.

#1 Player X1 serves a crisp ground ball to Y1; #2 Y1 attacks the goal above; #3 Y1 beat X1 and shoots at goal. The same action takes place for each pair at all 5 cone stations. On the next round Y1 serves to X1 who is now the defender instead of the attacker. After each has had an opportunity to attack from a given station, players move left one station and repeat the process at all 5 stations. If defender wins ball they score on the counter goals.

If necessary, limit attackers to 7 touches or whatever number you feel is appropriate. We never want players to get in the habit of attacking the goal 1v1 thinking that they have all the time in the world to make a move and shoot. Shooters who miss the goal retrieve their own ball. Do not be concerned if as the exercise continues there are two groups on the same cone station--players will work it out. It is good experience for them to learn how to accomplish the task without constantly having the coach solving all the problems.

Be certain that players keep score. You can also have players divided into two teams and have a team winner. Females are often reluctant to keep score and try to avoid revealing the winner. Request exact scores. Generally three rounds with each player having two attacks from each location are about right. If you decide to continue further, consider changing partners, winners against winners.

Multiple groups going at the same time is not a problem. Actually it offers a form of token defense such as an exemplary cover player in regular matches.

Dribble over the opposite Goal Line

Grid about 15 x 15 yards

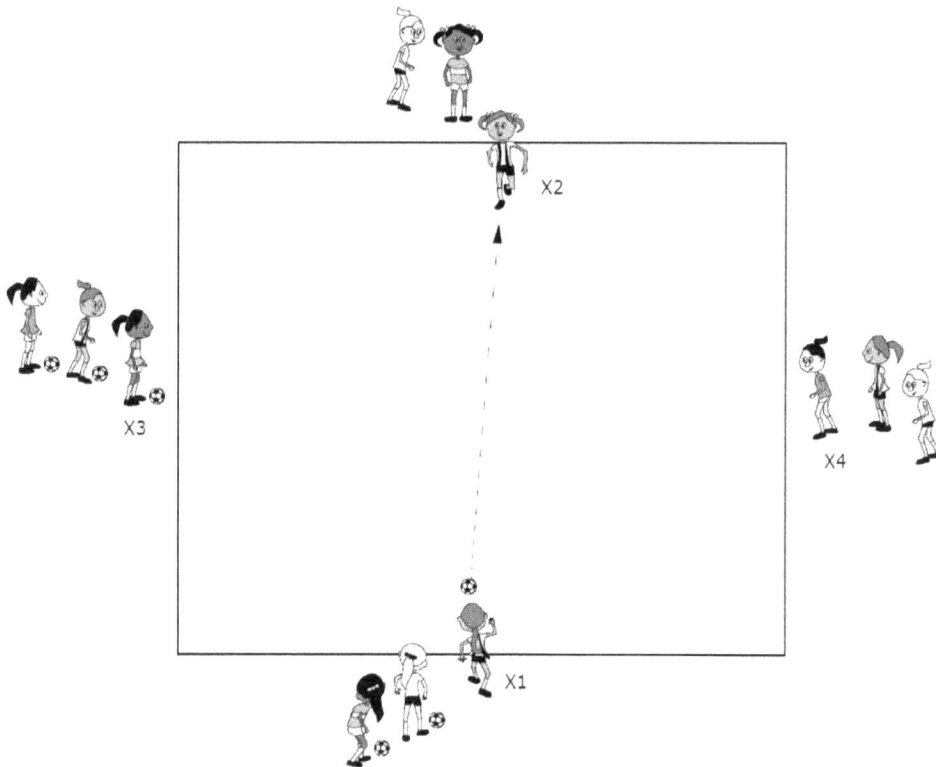

X1 serves a crisp ground ball to X2 and defends against her. X2 attempts to dribble over the opposing endline with an 8 touch restriction. All rotations are clockwise. If defender wins the ball she simply attacks the opposite goal line. No matter what occurs, the rotation is still the next original clockwise station from where a player was. Then X3 serve to X4 etc.

Be certain that no one goes to one of the serving lines without a ball. Try to insure many repetitions: two groups going at the same time is not a problem. It merely increases the visual development of players.

1 v 1 to Goal

Beginning Level: The coach is serving a neutral ball for two players to compete for.

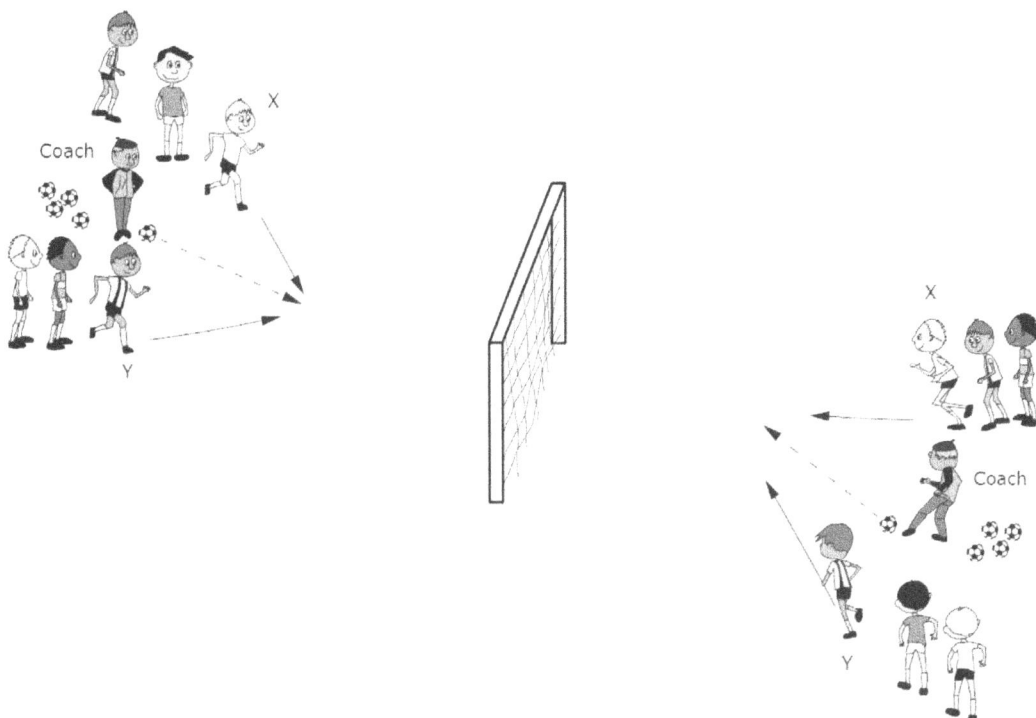

Possible scenario: On the left, player X from the top position won the ball, dribbled into the path of his opponent (a good strategy) and successfully shot the ball on goal. Whoever gets to the ball first shoots, the other attempts to defend. Players return balls to the coach.

Be certain the timing of service is unpredictable so that no player can leave before service. Occasionally even fake the pass. If one player is much faster you can give the other player one step forward or simply send the ball just a bit more into the path of the slower player. Note there are two groups working simultaneously. Flat faced goals are excellent for this activity, or if more than one goal is available, possibly two separate goals can be used accommodating two groups. With 8 or less players use one station.

Gate Keeper

Ed Holohan version: Two players, one from each line both start out dribbling around the cone toward the gate as shown. The first one through the gate is the shooter; the other is a defender who just leaves his ball in order to defend. Whichever team scores the most goals wins. The shooter retrieves all shots. On subsequent occasions place a goalkeeper in the goal. A second group can start as soon as the first pair goes around the corner cones. Be certain players take the shot on the first occasion that the shot is available.

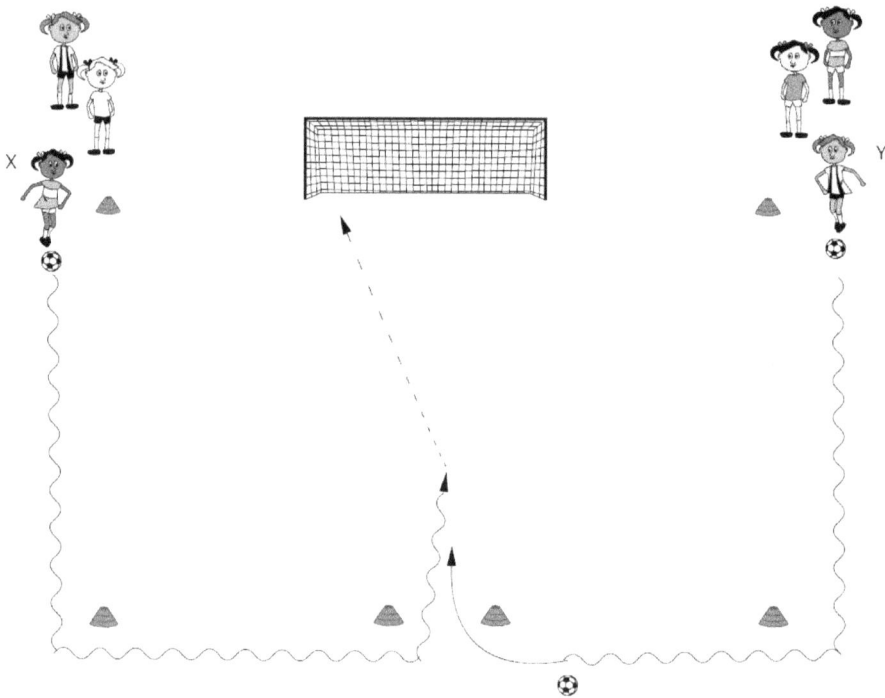

The speed dribble followed by control through the gate and then beating a defender is extremely game related. The entire area should be about 18x18 yards with the gate goal about 4 yards wide.

Baranello Fitness Shooting

The coach is about 25 yards away from the goal. Played with a keeper. The first player in each line upon the coach's signal "Go!" runs around the goal and tries to get to the ball served by the coach straight out about 15 yards away from the goal. The ball is served just as the players round the goal and are re-entering the field of play. Whoever wins the ball shoots at goal and the other player defends. The team with the most goals wins. The coach can make it a true 50/50 contest by where he serves the ball.

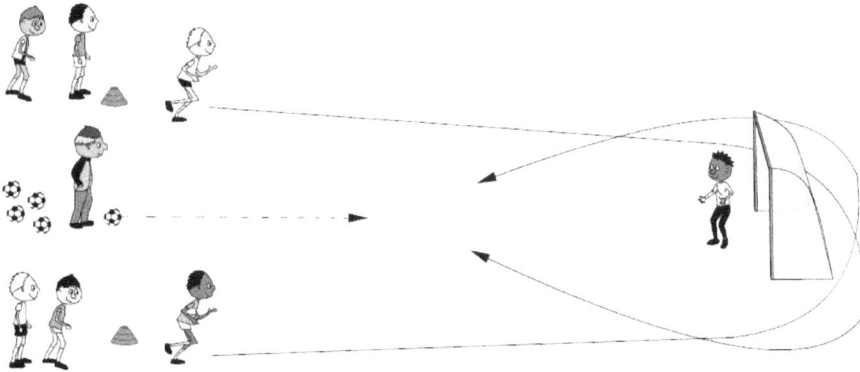

This is a fitness shooting activity that players truly enjoy! Some things amaze us coaches even after many years of experience. Played with or without a keeper. With large number of players, 16 or more, consider two groups.

'Half court Basketball'

In this case 1v1 soccer. Up to 5 pairs can work on a single goal. The groups simply provide additional defense for each other. Place four cones about 18 yards from the goal so that when the defender wins the ball she has to take the ball out past the cones. Once she is out past the 18 yard line, she turns and is now an attacker. What is good about this is that the players are attacking a real goal instead of cones or flags. No keeper is permitted since the possibility of two players shooting at the same time could cause injury to the keeper. Another possibility with this game is 2v2.
Option: Defenders when they win the ball have to go over the sideline of the penalty area.

This is often played as a scrimmage game using the whole team. Anywhere from 3v3 through 8v8 is effective. This can be more effective than the typical 6v4 or whatever in which the offense keeps getting the ball and defense defends. It also provides much more game reality, especially concerning rapid transition which is such an important element to success in the team game of soccer. In the team version Barry Gorman of Penn State often emphasized combination play in going to goal. This is clearly for more accomplished groups. The team version has a keeper in goal.

No matter what your philosophy or general thoughts are about the game of soccer, there is no question that developing young players to take on opponents with confidence is a skill of enormous importance. Naturally, we cannot expect it to be well developed unless we provide a great deal of practice in this vital skill.

SUPPORT

Support is the offensive tactic of being available to receive a pass from a teammate. Unquestionably this is one of the most basic and important tactical skills of the game. Generally, teams try to have at least one player behind the ball at a useful passing distance from the ball carrier. Useful distance means far enough away so the player pressuring the ball cannot cover the ball carrier and the support player, and close enough for an easy pass to be made and received. For youth one would think this distance generally is 7 to 14 yards, for older players somewhat further. Of course it is helpful to have a player forward of the ball in order to take some pressure off the ball carrier. With support somewhat clarified, the main issue is what are some good competitive fun exercises for accomplishing support?

Support can be clarified well in a 3v3 exercise where the team must dribble over the endline employing a grid about 15x18 yards. The main point for the coach to point out is that the ball carrier has a penetrating player forward of the ball and one slightly diagonally behind the ball for support. At first do this as a walk through with the players adjusting to that shape every time the ball is passed from one player to another.

#1 Xa passes to Xb, #2 Db stepped up to mark Xb and Xa dropped back to support Xb, #3 Da has moved to cover for Db who is now marking Xb.
Recalling that pressure and cover precedes marking; Db is initially properly positioned in case Xa beats Da. Xb is in an excellent support position and Xc is attempting to provide a penetrating pass option.
Hopefully Xc is constantly checking, blind siding Dc and in general is making every attempt to get free for a forward pass.

Actually this triangular concept of a support player is the same concept for any number of players in games, including 11 aside matches.

Possibly the only down side of 3v3 tournaments is that players must lean heavily toward man marking because due to the small field the goals are available for shots nearly all the time.

Note the larger spread of the attacking team while the defending team attempts to be compact to win the ball back. The coach must constantly encourage the attacking team to "Open up" in all playing situations as young players lack the patience to move away from the ball to provide support. This spreading out is often referred to as the **First Law of Offense**. It is very important to instill this behavior at an early age for long range player development. Generally it is not realistic to ask this until 8 to 10 years of age. See the section on team shape and passing/receiving inducements. Of course with the higher number of players there are generally two or more support players and often more than one penetrating player. Professionals can hit 60 yard balls accurately and so players many yards away from the ball carrier are constantly moving to support the ball even though they are very far away.

As always, move to an induced shortsided game using the whole team and award a point for every good support player movement. If desired, when numbers are 5 or more aside, you can deduct a point when the ball carrier has no support. This usually excludes the goalkeeper's support. End with unrestricted free play. Move from minimal coaching to no coaching in the unrestricted portion of the scrimmage.

Gate Goals Passing Support

On half of the age level's playing field have about eight 2 yards wide cone gate goals spread in random fashion. Players pair themselves up and the first pair to pass to their partners through all the gate goals win. This forces players to anticipate where the ball carrier can get to most quickly (easiest) and then be there ready to receive the partner's pass through the gate goal. Players must seek the more open areas in order to be successful.

For older ages of about ten or more try groups of three in order to start planting the advanced skill of third man-on which involves anticipating a second goal to go to while the two teammates are attacking a given gate goal. Discovery play method is perfect for achieving this goal. It is not necessary to instruct this idea, but when it occurs freeze the activity, compliment the group that did it, and then make them replay it under your guidance and explanation. Technically, third man-on is playing to third player on the first touch after a combination play such as a takeover, wall pass or overlap. However, for youth the previous simple idea more than suffices.

This activity can move to having a defender going around and knocking balls away. It can also progress to no defense with two teams each with their own ball and whichever team passes through five of the gate goals first wins. This could progress to allowing the opponents to defend by kicking an opponent's ball out of the area. Finally, simply play with two teams and one ball and whichever team passes the ball through 5 different gate goals first wins. Naturally one could start with the simple pairs and progress to one or two of the options and in this way have a whole session on support. This allows one field setup to be used without wasting time changing setups.

Gate Goal Passing is a great fun competitive game that teaches exactly what we want the players to learn by the game itself as opposed to coach-talk and explanation. That's real coaching! Designing an activity that teaches what you want players to learn instead of verbal instruction. This text includes dozens of such activities.

By all means compliment the groups who really start to work together and anticipate where to go next rapidly. Successful groups usually have good communication. If you note good communication, by all means recognize it to all the players. Many loud verbal sounds aren't always good communication. An example of "negative noise" is a player who is marked calling for the ball. Quality communication is positive, useful, productive conveyance of information! In this activity the player's position is a form of communication!

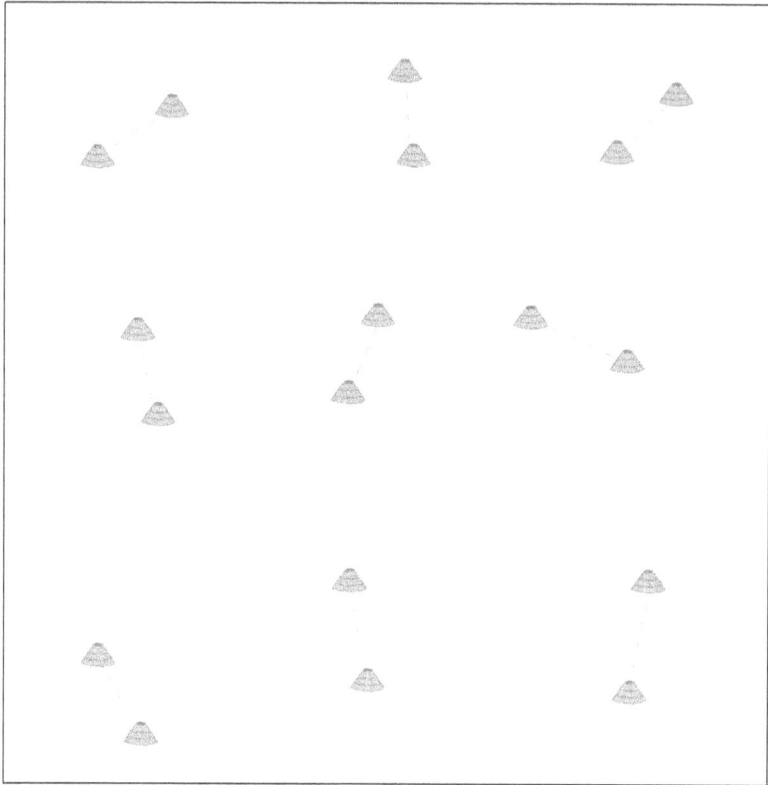

Here 7 to 10 gate goals randomly dispersed in a large grid can accommodate innumerable support, dribbling and passing/receiving fun games. Cones or poles both work well.

Grid Support

Support in a 10 yard grid, requiring thinking of the support position. Player A has the ball and there are two players, B and C, at the adjoining two cones. When A passes to B, C must move quickly so that B has 2 players at the two adjoining corners. When B passes to C, note A has moved in support of C. Often done with players as young as 6 years of age, but also with higher age levels.

This is an important pivotal activity that will require serious instruction. This activity can be repeated often so that support becomes an instinctual response as opposed to having to think about it. Then of course it is time to move to higher levels.

Essentially wherever the ball is, there must be players at the two adjoining cones!

It is best while the other coach is doing the dribbling to take three able players and have them firmed up in the activity to show it to the others. With young groups of 5-8 year olds it is best to instruct each group individually while the others dribble, juggle, shoot or scrimmage. Progress to a crab defender, which is close to no defense at all. Move to a defender who has her hands on her knees or behind her back. By about age 9 or 10 a true unrestricted defender playing 3v1 can be instituted. Instead of changing defenders every 3 minutes just have whoever loses the ball defend. Never allow players to wait until the defender is ready. Instead, passing/receiving should progress non-stop!

Dutch 4 Goal Game

The classic Dutch four goal game is widely used. Often referred to as the Dutch game only because it was popularized in the Netherlands. Wherever or whoever started using it is unknown. In any case it is an extremely important basic shortsided activity that promotes support, change in point of attack and many major concepts of soccer. Virtually all professional and accomplished youth coaches use this activity for the development of young players. For the young age levels the field is about 30 yards wide and 20 yards long so as to encourage its primary objective. That is, change in point of attack. Pugg goals are ideal for this activity.

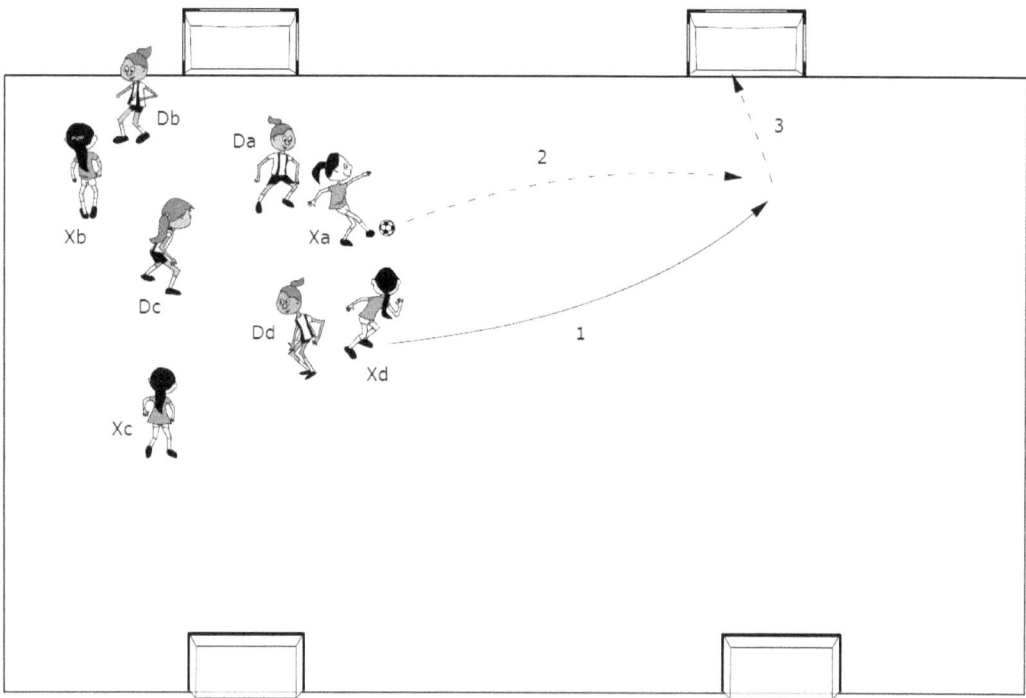

#1 Xd being somewhat astute realizes that instead of further crowding of the left side, that there is an easy goal to be scored at the right side goal. #2 Xa turns, sees and passes the ball to Xd. #3 Xd shoots and scores.

This is the discovery method at its best. Many coaches use this activity several times a month. It embodies all of the concepts of this text. Technical/tactical concepts, abundant ball touches, important skills of the game and much more. Best of all, players love this game!

Flat Faced Goal Game

This game has 2 teams attacking the flat faced goal. Teams attack the opposite side of the goal from wherever they win the ball. The ball must go OUTSIDE the cones as shown in the diagram when going from one side to the other. When defending right after a shot, we want the ball to go away from the goal quickly, and when it gets to the flank for the goal being attacked we want services. So you see how this is an excellent game which encourages passing.

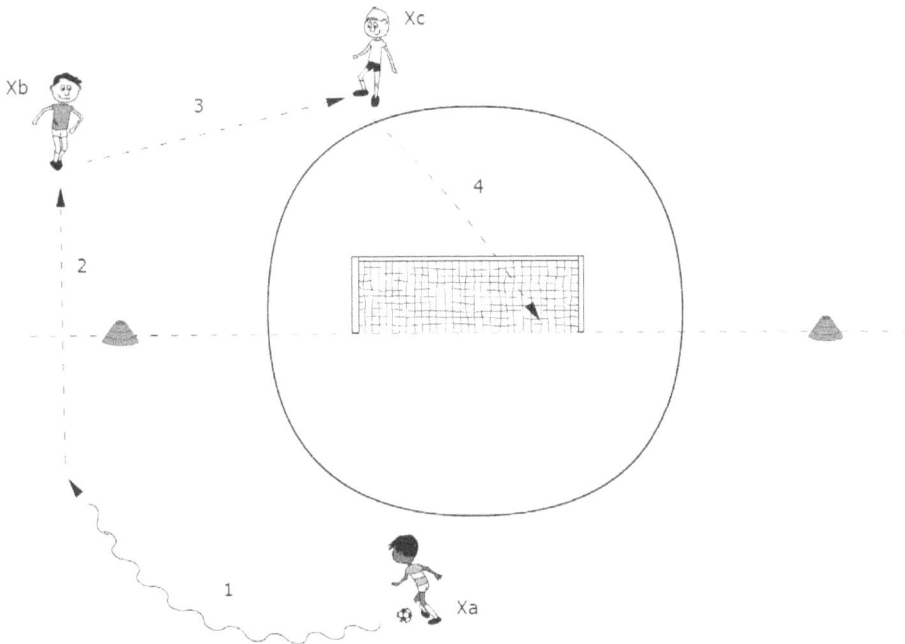

#1 Xa Wins the ball and dribbles out wide #2 Xa passes to teammate Xb on the other side #3 Xb sees Xc open and passes him the ball #4 Xc takes a shot on goal.

No one is permitted to stay in the circular area, which could be a field center circle or an area marked out by cones. Players only go into the restricted area to retrieve the ball and must immediately get it out of the circular area with a pass or dribble. The ball still must go around the distant cone.

Advanced Option: A possible passing inducement is requiring every player to touch the ball before going to goal. Winners retain possession and after scoring merely go to the opposite side to score again. There can be many varied wrinkles to this fun game in accordance with the coach's desired goal.

1 vs 1 Goal Area

In this 1v1 game, you must pass the ball to your teammate in the end area in order to score.

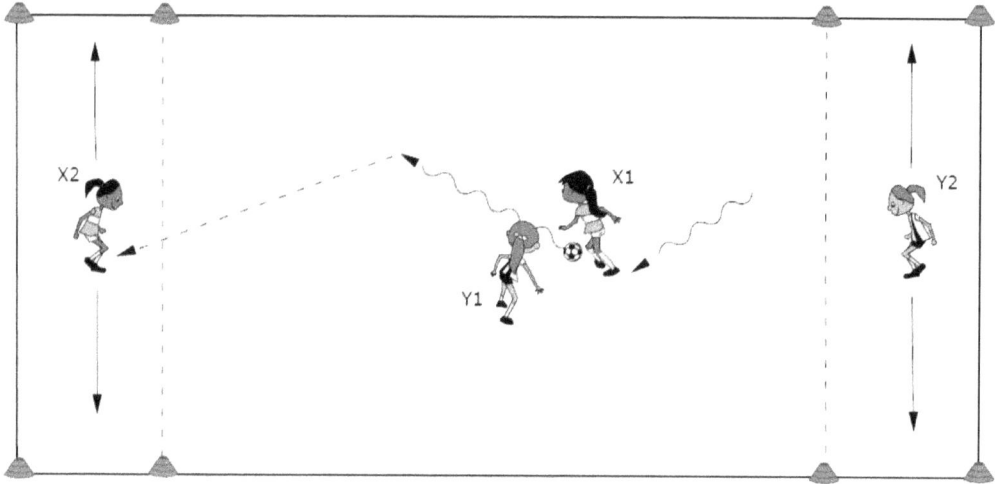

X1 and Y1 are playing a 1v1 game and score by passing to their teammate in the end area. When X1 has completed a pass to X2, X2 merely gives a free pass to Y1 who attacks in the opposite direction while X1 defends. Pairs change roles every two minutes.

Since this is being used for delivery to a target player, the main coaching emphasis is ensuring that X2 and Y2 in the end areas are moving in SUPPORT of their dribbling partner at all times. This means being in the most available area to receive a pass.

This could be a big area with various partners working in the same area.

To empower players, give them greater responsibilities. Even though it would be far from perfect, it would cause far greater learning to have players set up the areas, modeling theirs after the one the coach set up.
Option: Increase the end areas and have one player from each team in the end area forcing the target player to learn how to check, blind side a defender and/ or provide a side-on bump to get free.

Changing the Point of Attack

In this exercise the ball is played wide and then must be passed into the central grid area to the neutral player. Generally the neutral player must play the ball wide again. Now the ball goes back to the area in front of the goal for a score. This exercise could be anything from 3v3 up to 6v6.

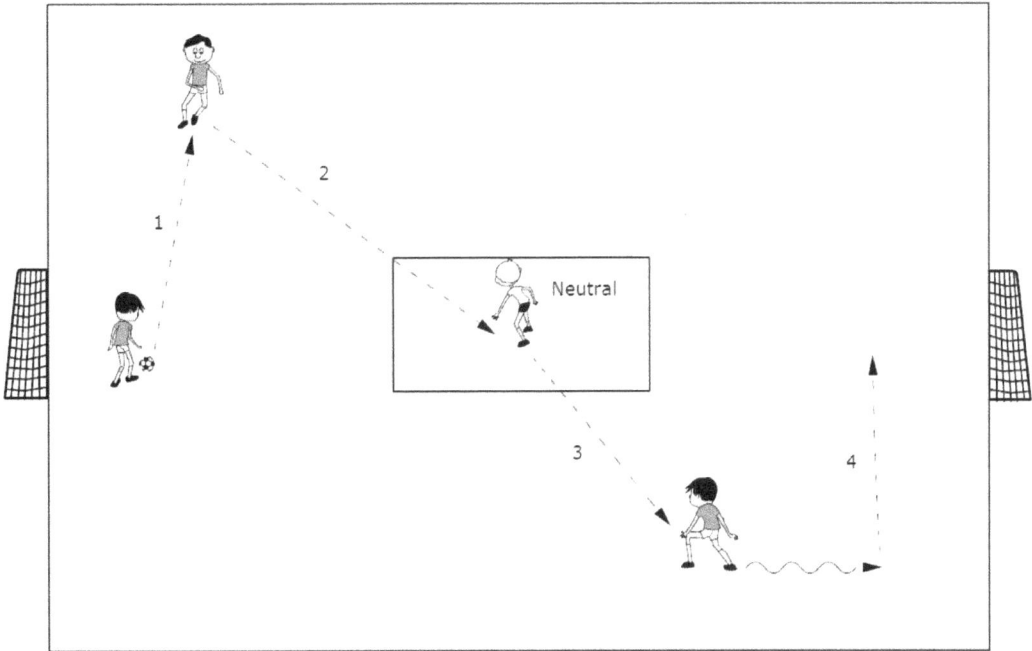

While the movement of the ball in the diagram is very idealistic, it certainly can occur if trained for and would result in minimal energy expenditure for the offense and a great deal of effort required of the defense. This exercise fosters 'opening up of the hips', creates vision of teammates and defenders to facilitate good decisions. Often the neutral is a center middie offensive player often referred to as the schemer. A schemer is a central midfielder who often sets up goal scoring opportunities. Two teams with a ball going both ways simultaneously; then play competitively with one ball going in a single direction.

Option: No use of neutral player, but a teammate must go into this area after the ball is passed----still there is no defending in the neutral area.

This inside/out, outside/in change in point of attack movement facilitates purposeful possession for creating scoring chances.

This activity can be done with as few as 7 players and as many players as you have on your team. Simultaneously this trains the central middie to change the point of attack, which is so valuable for attaining game success. High level teams make great efforts to prevent the ball from getting into this general area. It is sometimes referred to as the staging area. In any case it is dangerous because balls going wide from this area require defenders to move out wide and while that is happening dangerous crosses or even a through ball becomes a major concern. In this simple exercise young players are gaining experience in a technical/tactical domain of great importance to success at high levels of play.

POWER INSTEP DRIVE

With the positive proliferation of shortsided games in recent years, which is a great improvement over the inane eleven aside games for ages 7-11, the power instep drive quality has deteriorated. On the positive side, skill development has improved enormously due to the abundance of shortsided training and games. On the flip side, few players can strike a ball with power due to the fact that shortsided play seldom requires the power instep drive. Unfortunately, when we had the very young age groups playing 11-aside many youngsters could strike a ball far distances, but the game was chaotic kick and run. Sometimes this was a toe kick instead of a power instep drive, and the fact that many of the ball strikes were kicks to nowhere instead of passes, crosses, shots or quality services was an unhappy circumstance. In any case there is a serious need for the power instep drive for shooting, crosses, long passes, direct kicks, big changes in point of attack and occasionally for defensive clearances.

What are the major components of the power instep drive? What are some of the activities that will develop this vital skill?

Among the many technical aspects of the power instep drive the following are primary:
- Lock the ankle down: to achieve this, it helps to press toes to bottom of shoe.
- Strike the ball with the laces; often a bit to the inside portion of the laces; have players put their finger right on the correct spot and go around to see that they know the correct area. There is a hard bone there. In practical terms it is the area between the ankle and the toes. Many players have the shoe laces knot at this very location, which is not a good idea. For this reason many high level players place the knot on the side, sometimes by wrapping laces around the bottom of their cleats.

Balls struck with the white area indicated have an excellent chance of having good pace. If the vertical center is struck or even an inch above center the power instep drive will have a good chance of being on goal or other destination.

- Non-kicking foot should be about 5 inches (varies greatly with age of player) away from the side of the ball and pointing to the intended location.
- Look at your target, exact location you want the ball to go, but see the ball when you strike it.
- Knee directly over the ball; the power instep kick to some extent is a two part motion of planting the non-kicking foot and bringing the knee over the ball, and then releasing all the power from the knee.
- Show that when your knee is up over the ball you will not stub your foot, which hurts a great deal and can cause injury. This is done by standing with the knee lifted and sending the foot back and forth showing that it never hits the ground. Also show how the foot hits the ground when the knee is not lifted.

Note with a proper knee lift the toe area of the soccer cleat does not reach the ground. This allows the player to approach the ball at a slight angle, have a follow through to the target and achieve maximum power. Naturally in an actual kick the non-kicking foot would be closer to the ball.

By contrast note without a proper knee lift the player's foot would stub the ground causing injury and/or severe pain.

- Approach the ball at a modest angle of about 15 degrees; 50 to 90 degrees is not good; in fact this is why so many players cannot drive a ball and think that a spinning counter clockwise strike is okay when in fact it is a serious loss of power. This bad habit of approaching the ball from a serve angle also often causes a poor follow through and loss of accuracy.

- Approach the ball at a modest speed, rhythmically; this sometimes requires a stutter step.
- For proper follow-through land on the kicking foot. Even if at later stages of development many players do not do this, for early ages of instruction this helps youngsters acquire a proper follow through.

The earlier mention of training the habit of proper ball preparation especially comes into prominence with the power instep drive

POWER INSTEP DRIVE PROGRESSION

Tap a ball with knee lifted so as not to hit the ground; ball held by coach and/or teammate in pairs. Sit on the ground and tap the ball in the air with the ankle FIRMLY locked down. Stand and strike a still ball at a fence, flat faced goal, kicking wall, brick or cement block wall, outdoor handball court (any surface which stops the ball, allowing much repetition in a short period of time) or if necessary work with partners at an appropriate distance apart for the age level. Move to prepare the ball and then strike it, generally 65% power. Some research shows maximum accuracy is achieved when using about 65% power. A simple definition of power is a combination of speed and strength. For young players the prepare distance is usually about one or two yards, and preparing the ball at a slight angle. Focus on form before power. Move to receive, prepare, followed by power instep drive to intended location. After several sessions try to have players receive, turn/prepare and strike the ball after a turn. Progress to checking two or three steps to the ball, receive/turn-prepare/strike the ball.

Throughout all the instruction emphasize keeping the ball LOW and having a specific intended location (target).

Striking a Moving Ball

Four players as seen in the diagram.

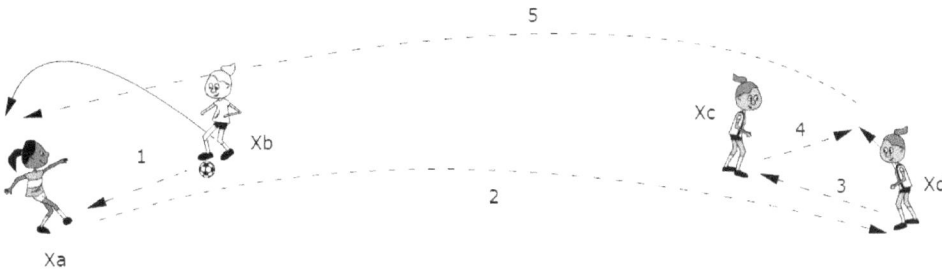

#1 Xb lays off a very slow ground ball to Xa's strong kicking foot; #2 Xa delivers a one touch long ball to Xd; #3 Xd receives and lays off to Xc; #4 Xc lays it back to Xd; #5 Xd strikes it to Xb who is now in Xa's location. Many high level teams use this as part of their game warm-up.

Xa and Xb exchange places, as do Xc and Xd on each successive trial. Adjust the distance between players according to the level of the players. Always allow plenty of space between the two players on each side, as small spaces require near perfect passes in order to execute the exercise effectively.

Some activities to firm up the power instep kick are shooting from a distance, crossing activities, and long ball services to receiving strikers. Practice at a kicking wall. See Circle Shooting in the shooting section and require the shot from behind a cone placed the appropriate distance for a long shot on goal. All shots are taken from behind the designated cone.

Knocking Down the Crows

Beginning Level: For the very young ones this is excellent. Have about 15 standup cones; each team must 'shoot' (knock) down the 'crows' (cones) from behind the line. Lines can be marked with danger marking tape, cones, rope, string, or lines on the field.

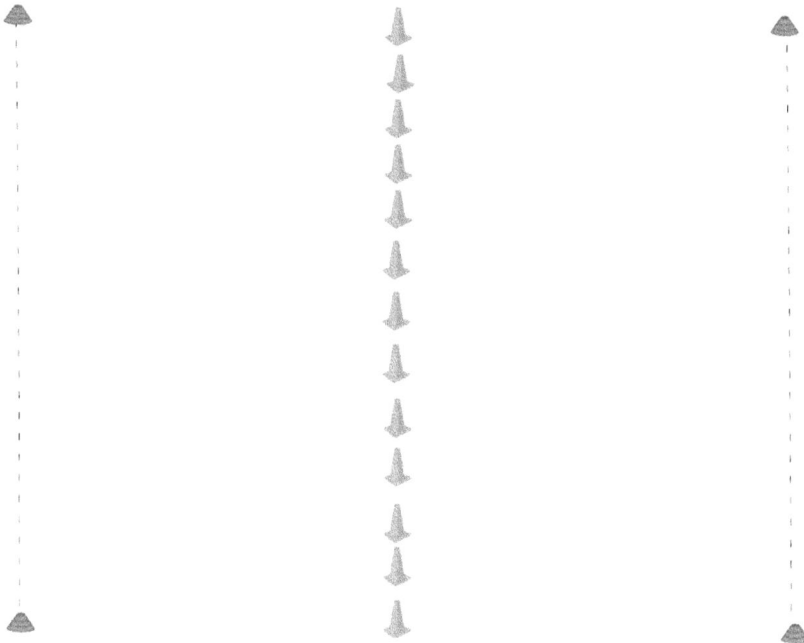

The team that has knocked down the most cones when all are knocked down wins. The area between the lines from which players must shoot can only be used to retrieve balls. All shots at the cones are from behind the line that is about 15 yards from the cones. Violators' team loses a point. If available about 15 cones works best.

Often it is best to have a parent or assistant coach count the number of cones one team knocked down, and the regular coach count for the other team. Of course, if the regular coach is alone all he needs to do is count how many cones one team knocks down, knowing that all the other cones were knocked down by the other team. Motivation is very high for this game. Make sure that nearly everyone gets involved in retrieving the balls that leave the area and setting up the cones for the next trial.

SHORTSIDED GAMES

Shortsided games are important because they:
- Increase the number of touches, which is critical to muscle memory
- Generally are 'positionless' (there are no positions)
- Require everyone to play offense, defense and active transition
- Are fun
- Allow ball and game to teach the skills of soccer
- Involve many 1v1 and tackling situations
- Have very high fitness demands
- Provide many goal scoring opportunities

Simply, shortsided games teach soccer in a manner that motivates players to continue to learn and play the game. Shortsided games foster both the technical and tactical elements of the game while the fitness component gets right to the big picture of a child's development----a healthy mind in a healthy body!

The basic four goals "Dutch" training game has already been clarified previously and is only mentioned here because it is a fundamental shortsided game to be used for all ages. It requires almost no talk, can be set up in a minute or two and is invaluable for having players learn possession and change in point of attack in a fun game format. It has innumerable valuable purposes. Incidentally it is excellent for defensive purposes as well.

Moving Goals

Moving goals is a game using a pool noodle, best with a rope threaded through the center. Two teams attempt to score on the two players manning the moving goal. The goal must remain full sized at all times, but can be moved anywhere in the grid to prevent either team from scoring. Change the goal movers regularly. Coaches could be the goal movers.

Here the lime team and the rainbow team (non-vested players) are competing to score goals. It looks like our two coaches did not move fast enough to deny a goal. Note how taut the goal is----the two goal tenders are absolutely required to keep the goal full sized. When using players to be goal tenders make this requirement totally clear!

Option 1: Two moving goals and either team can score on either goal; goal movers try to deny all scoring.

Option 2: Two moving goals, two teams, and each team has a ball and tries to score on the goal manned by the opponents. Sub-options: No defending by field players of the goal

Option 3: Teams may defend by kicking the other team's ball out of the area. There are many possible options to this activity.

In previous eras this game was played with a broom stick or similar pole, but the safety and liability issues of the modern era make that out of the question. A hard object such as a stick can cause a child to be hit in the eye, causing serious injury.

Keeper Wars

In this popular game, two keepers with two full sized goals or goals of the age level about 25 yards apart attempt to score on each other. It can be a totally open game using any throwing or kicking skill or a demand for only: punts, goal kicks, underhand throws, overhead throws, dribbling or must dribble past opponent. The same game can be played by field players using dribbling and shooting. For even more fun, play 1 v 1 plus keepers, or 2 v 2. The down side is it requires two full sized goals for the age level, but once the coach learns to have different groups doing different things (an advanced coaching skill), this is a great fun skill builder for either the keepers or field players. While the team is doing the instruction for the day (the possession activity, a shortsided game, etc.) two players at all times can be on the two goals, possibly for 10 minute time periods. This is another reason to have an assistant; he/she could do the timing, calling two players at a time and the supervising the 'war' game.

This is a wonderful activity to keep in mind for the day when only 2-6 players show up for training. Sometimes when there are so few players there is a lack of enthusiasm and this is a tremendously motivating activity to bring life to your training session!

It appears that Megan has drilled a ball past Nick for a score. This is also an excellent game for field players for dribbling and shooting!

Open Goal, Closed Goal

Four corner goals shortsided game is outstanding for vision development and decision making.

Set up the grid as shown, about 20x30 yard size adjusted to number of players. Anything from 2v2 to 6v6 with four players at the four corner cone goals works well. Four neutrals are stationed one near each cone goal and follow the coach's command to enter or leave the goal. With a low number of players simply have only 3 or 2 gate goals.

For 2v2 with 4 neutrals, eight players are required, for 3v3 ten players are required and so forth. The coach signals with a simple hand motion to the neutral player near a goal; that means go into the goal. When the neutral player is in the goal and receives a signal from the coach that means step out of the goal. The essence of the game is that when the goal is closed, it is not a goal. The coach can have all four goals open, or 1, 2 or 3 open. When all four goals are closed it obviously is a possession game. Due to the coach's control of the game he/she can always have the score be very competitive. The last 3 minutes of the game the coach does not change the number of open goals, and so a true deserving winner gets the victory. Change the players near the goals about every 4 minutes. In this way all get to play and also rest.

3 V 1 Shortsided Game

3v1, on a field 15 x 20 yards with 3 players on each team. At all times the defending team has a player on each endline that can only defend the endline by remaining along the line. In the playing area the game is 3v1 with an offensive player required to dribble over the end line to score. Play 4 rounds of 4 minutes each, alternating teams on each successive round. In this way every player will have had at least one turn to be the defender.

The X's are trying to penetrate forward in attempt to dribble over the left side endline. If Y1 wins the ball she just passes to her teammate Y2. Then three Y's attack a single X, the other two X's are on each goal line After each score the opponents go on the attack. Extra balls can be behind the goal lines or at the coach's feet.

Play six rounds. The winning team after six rounds is the team with the most goals. All play is restarted with the ball being awarded to the three attackers.

If necessary adjust the size of the field to facilitate offensive success. Wider will definitely help the team in possession.

Coaching points are maintaining the triangular shape with significant spread out spacing. Feinting to penetrate along one side and then attempting to score on the opposite side will facilitate scoring. Compliment the team that first uses this tactic!

3 V 3 Shortsided Game

In an area of 15 by 25 yards with 3 players on each team, one player must defend the endline "goal". Dribbling over the goal line or passing to a teammate over the goal line scores a goal. As soon as the ball is lost one player moves back to the goal line, assuming the 'keeper' role. In these situations where any one of the players assume a passive role, encourage players to alternate such a role.

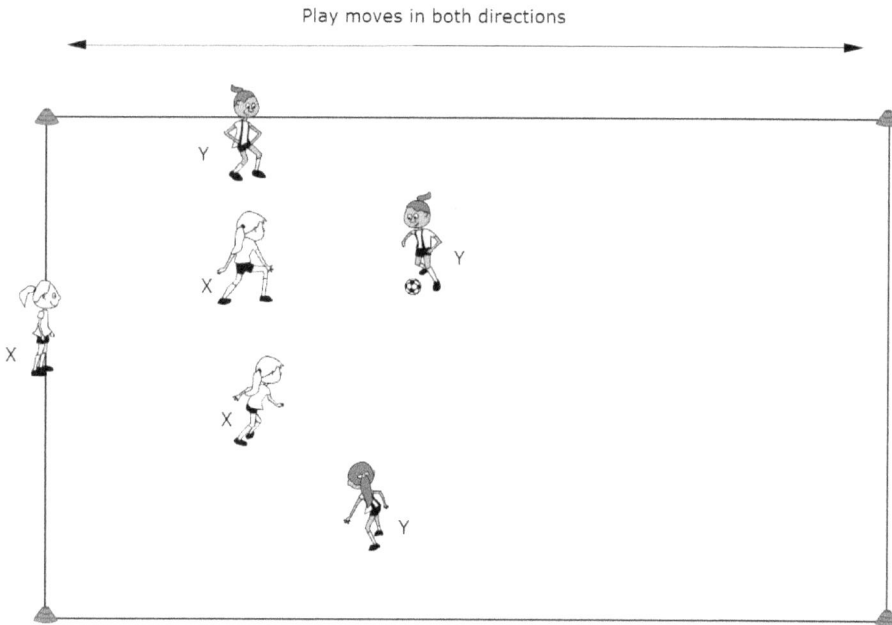

Play moves in both directions

Y

Y

X

X

X

Y

3 v 3 Playing Wide

In this instance the ball must go through either of the side gates. Often the area is as wide or even wider than it is long. An area of 30 yards wide and 25 long will accommodate most groups. This game also helps to break up the bee swarm a bit, as players must use the perimeter of the field.

In this case, a regular game of 3v3 is played with the simple demand that the ball crossing the midline must pass through one of the gate goals.

Having a neutral player will greatly facilitate success and many teams have an advanced level player who can fill this role. It fills the dual role of further developing the advanced player since she may well be ready to move from the "I, me" dribbling stage to the passing stage of development. Neutrals help the team in possession and move all over the playing area to support play, but generally cannot score.

3 V 3 Tournament

This always makes a practice session of great interest. Still do a warm-up to get numerous ball contact and technical development. With three teams the coach can work with the waiting group while the other two teams play. Winners stay on. With 4 teams it simply becomes winners against winners. Number of players need not be equal, but teams must be of equal strength. The alternative is to have subs, but no one stays out of the game for more than 2 minutes. Games should be 8-10 minutes. If the tournament ends early simply add a shooting activity. Generally field size is about 20 x 30 yards.

I once tried to postpone a scheduled 3v3 Tournament session and the player response was so strong I decided that it was an unwise decision!

2 V 2 with 3 players on each team

One player remains on each goal line. A point is scored with a successful pass to the end line player if he gains control of the ball.

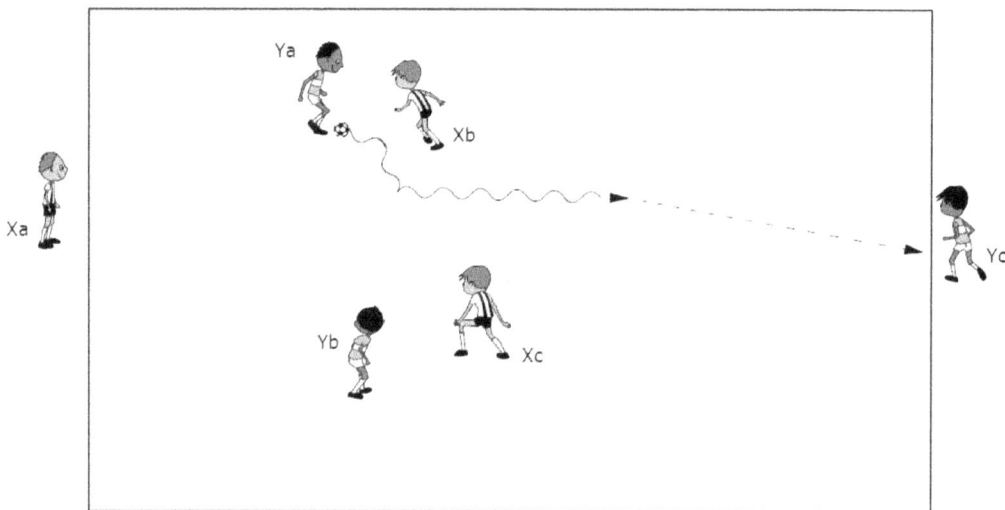

The Ya player at the top of the grid has just scored by passing to the end line teammate Yc.

Clearly this simple game leads up to being able to pass to the striker. In the 11 v 11 this is often labeled as a target player. If the coach chooses, the rudiments of defense can be included. Note Xc is laying back for cover in case the ball is lost. This type of instruction should only begin after players are somewhat successful with controlling the ball with dribbling and passing/receiving. If the offense cannot successfully keep the ball, pass and occasionally hit the target player there is no point in focusing on the defense.

3 Goals, 3 Teams

Flag goals are 4 yards wide. A fun game with greatly increased passing and dribbling in a large grid; half of a field, with three teams each having one flag goal to defend.

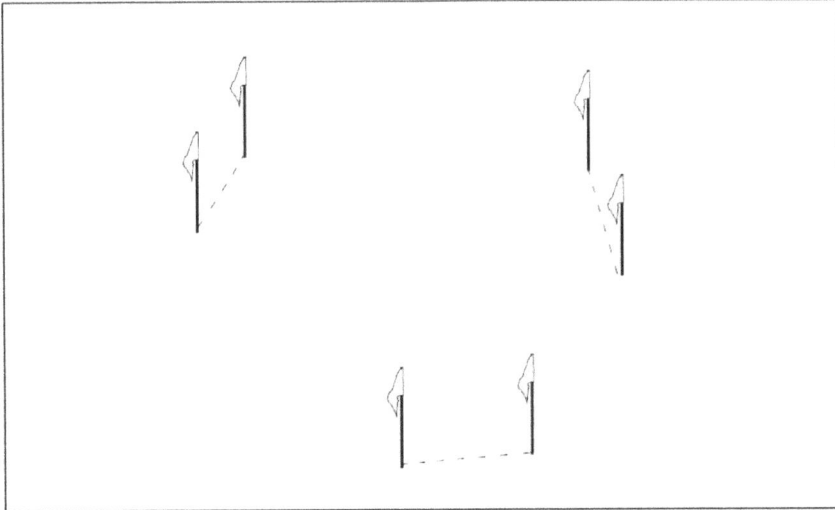

Each team attacks the other two teams' goals. Scoring can be from either direction. Can be played with a keeper-sweeper. First team with 5 goals wins or play to a period of time. Five minute rounds might be about right.

Make even teams, but teams do not have to have equal numbers. It's hard to find a game with more visual demands. Don't be surprised if players ask for this game regularly.

Option: Two teams, score on any goal, defend all goals. This could also use a single triangle goal.

Kings Game

Kings Game is an exciting 4v4 (or anything from 2 to 6 a-side) fast paced finishing game that involves transition. It is enjoyed by all players from age ten to adults.

The field is 25 yards long by 50 yards wide. It is played with 3 or 4 teams and two goalkeepers. Here four teams are shown.

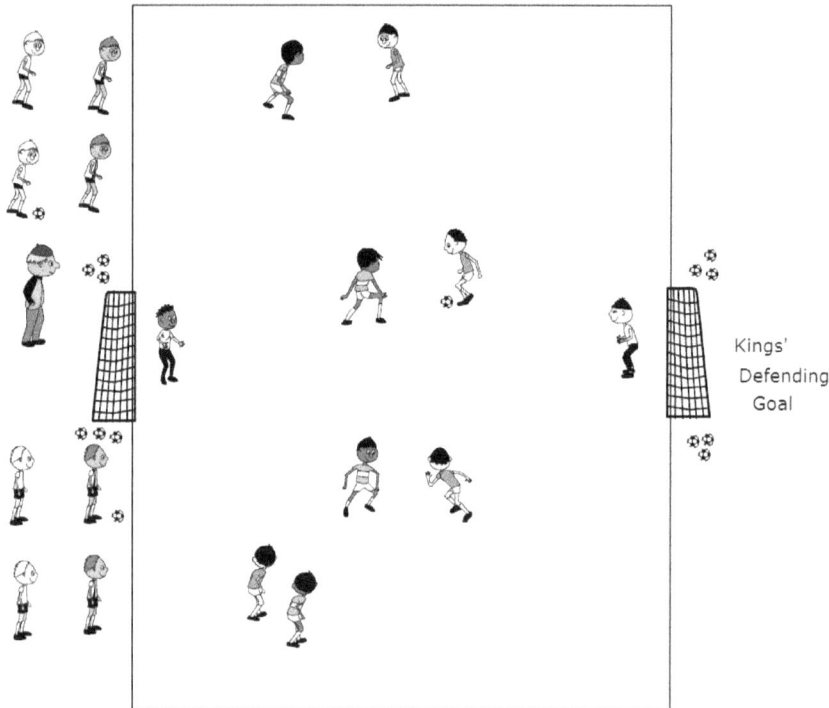

Kings'
Defending
Goal

The Orange team on the right is the Kings team, has the ball, and are attacking the left side goal. The Lime team is defending. If Kings (orange) score they remain Kings and Lime leaves immediately and gets back in line behind the white team. Blue who has a ball at one player's feet, dribbles onto the field to attack the Kings (right) side. Orange must recover to defend instantly.

If Lime wins the ball and scores they switch over to the Kings side and blue team attacks Lime. Extra balls are placed outside each post so anytime the ball goes out-of-bounds, the keeper quickly puts a ball in play..

The only time a new team comes onto the field is when a goal is scored!
Note that teams lined up to come onto the field always have one player with a ball ready to attack immediately.

Whenever a shot is taken that is not on goal the shooter must go and retrieve the ball quickly as that team must play shortsided until that individual retrieves the ball and gets back on the field.

The Kings Game is an excellent game for keepers to deal with goalmouth chaos and numerous shots. The winning team is the team that scored the most goals after 25 minutes. The coach may have difficulty changing to another activity due to the desire of players to continue; therefore it is best to do this activity at the end of the session.

If two teams are on for a long period without scoring, you can just pick a team to rotate off or take out the keepers until a goal is scored.

A two minute walk through should allow teams to learn the game very quickly. This is especially true because as soon as they get the idea of the excitement and fun of the game, players try hard to learn the rules as quickly as possible.

Channel Play

This game is often used for encouraging crossing and having other players be in locations to finish the crosses. This can be used for many different purposes besides crossing, such as wall passes, overlaps, changes in point of attack and many more strategies the coach chooses to develop.

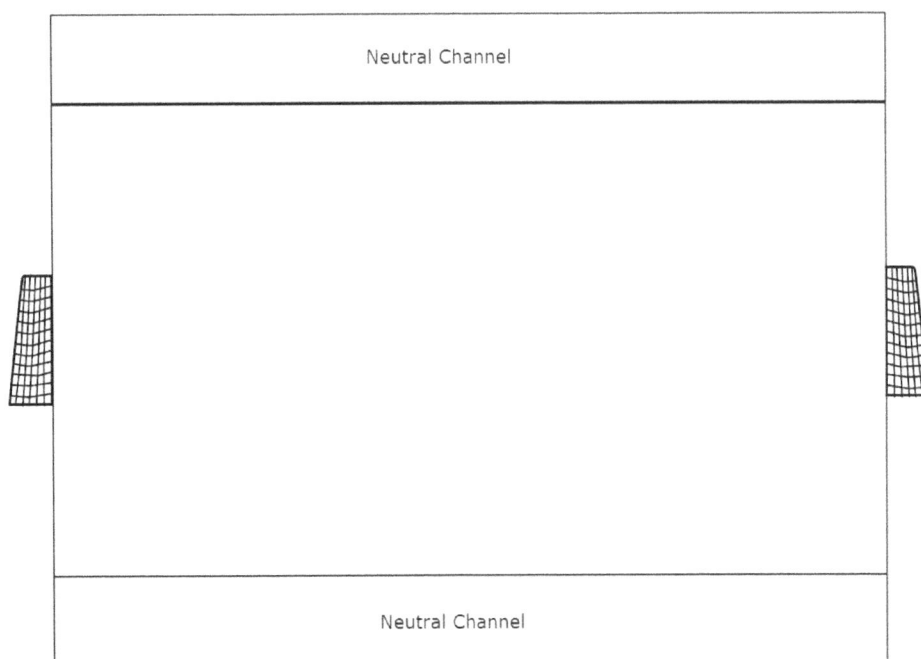

Whatever the channel is used for there is no defending in the channel. Here the game is a regular game with a neutral wing in each channel that dribbles endline and crosses the ball to whichever team gave her the ball. The requirement is that a cross must occur before going to goal. Generally played with keepers and full squads (10 to 22 players). Age 9 and older.

Neutrals for shortsided games and scrimmages of the whole team are also great facilitators for achieving a given instructional goal. Invariably neutrals can only play offense. Neutrals can be:

- A single player or even two or more
- On or off the field playing area
- Used in possession exercises as well as for shortsided games
- Can be defended against or not defended against
- Neutrals usually don't defend

Neutrals are often chosen to perform the role they play in the actual game: Winger as server, midfield schemer setting up goals, wingback overlapping, etc.

If nothing else this kind of activity opens up the field. Recalling that offense wants to spread out a defense, this certainly will help the team to make use of the whole field.

At higher levels there are often defenders in the channel, but still allowing increased offense by having two offensive players and one defender.

3 v 1 Hit the Cone

3v1 Hit the Cone has a grid of 20 x 20 yards with a 3 yard grid at its center. At the center of the grid is a large cone or an upright cone that the 3 offensive players must hit to score. Sometimes played with a ball on top of a cone. Every two minutes the defender is changed and the player that allowed the least number of goals is the winner. While this is mostly an offensive passing/ receiving possession game that demands changes in point of attack, it just simply is a lot easier to keep score by the goals yielded by the defender. This is likely a game for age 9 and above, but that always depends on the ability of the players.

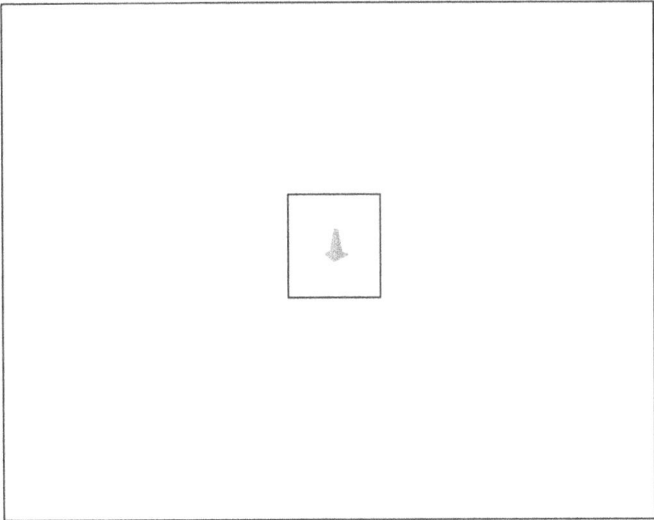

Options: 4v1, 5v2, and any other combination of players the coach chooses as long as she creates a fair challenge for both sides.

3 v 3 Klivecka

3v3 Klivecka is simply played with a team dribbling over the endline. Area of 12 x 20 yards with any of the following as emphasis are in order: dribbling, passing/receiving, support, cover, triangle play, steering, simple penetration of having a forward player, checking, opening up when in possession, pressing the ball and dozens of other worthy topics. Its main purpose is to clarify the offensive roles of penetration/support/mobility and defensive roles of pressure/cover/balance. However, only one particular role is emphasized in a single session. The following diagrams show some of the many possibilities of this simple format.

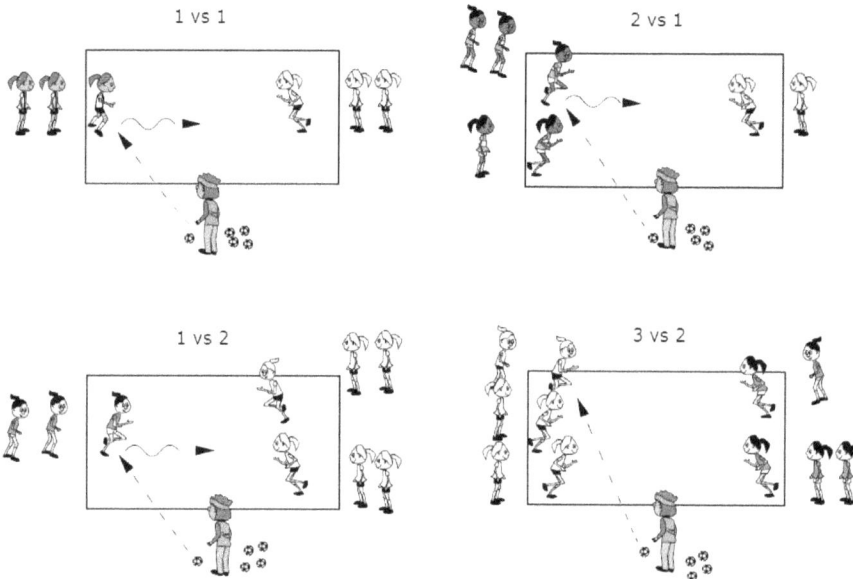

Players are merely placed outside the grid in accordance to the number of players to be used in the activity. The coach serves a ball.

As you can see this structure works well for 1v1, 1v2, 2v1, 2v2, 2v3, 3v2 and 3v3. My two favorites are 1v2 and 2v3, both used for teaching pressure/cover. It is also excellent for support using 2v1. However, this environment is so flexible that it can accommodate many different concepts of the game.

3v3 is very rigorous so it can easily accommodate 10 players with constant changing of roles. Usually a simple clockwise rotation works fine. With the uneven numbers, players have to use judgment and go to the location that is in need of players. The grid for 3v3 obviously is larger. Brief coaching points are an essential part of this 3v3 format. Another very common use is for wall passes and rear support.

106

GENERAL PEDAGOGY

<u>Passive Defenders</u> are not recommended in this text because no one knows what 50%, 75% or 90% passive means. Children least of all grasp such a difficult idea. Furthermore, we spend so much time trying to make situations game related, and passive defending erodes full effort. The preferred method is restrictions on the defender such as: crab defender, hands on head, hands behind back, hands on knees, reduced number of defenders, multiple balls, space restrictions, no defense until the pattern of receiving/passing has been established.

Establishing the pattern using multiple groups in the same area, each with their own ball, but not defending against each other is excellent for learning a given idea. Once players can implement the tactic then a single ball is used. The latter method has come into prominence in recent years and makes a lot of sense by saving a lot of training time. The two ball technique with both groups working in the same area provides a low level kind of defense, increases ball touches and is a great time saver. It allows the pattern or whatever the coach is teaching to have success before facing a more active defense. It is not unusual for advanced coaches to use this technique nearly every practice. This methodology was widely promulgated by Wayne Harrison.

As coaches we must demand maximum effort and rapid transition, rather than a lackadaisical attitude. This method accomplishes good defending by demanding quality footwork, while 'passive' defending can only contribute to the develoment of bad habits. 50% effort is not tolerated in the match, so why ask for it in training?

Endline Neutrals

While end line neutrals are common for learning how to attack a goal, especially by encouraging achieving the end line and sometimes for heading purposes, the arrangement presented here varies greatly from other sources. Note in the diagram the placement of 'endline neutrals' is not beyond the field of play as many sources place such players. Here the endline players are on the field, which increases their vision, offsides understanding (even though in these types of games the offside law is not maintained) and of course is much more realistic in terms of being game related.

This shows the general area of movement for the neutrals to create goals. Later on when there is a live defense, they are allowed to score goals as well as create shots.

A common game of anywhere from 4v4 to 8v8 with keepers often has neutral players off the field beyond the goal line. These players are restricted to a single touch. One touch service for both ground and air balls (including chips for heading) are still accomplished, but here the player plays a much more active role, being able to constantly move vertically and horizontally in about a five yard area just as a player might do during a competitive match. In this way not only are shots being promoted, but also the neutrals are gaining a better understanding of the movements necessary to create goals. Eventually reality is brought into play by running the same activity but enforcing the offsides law. Players also get away from the notion that the goal can be successfully attacked using only one or two players, when in reality good teams often have 3 to 5 or more players directly involved for successful strikes at goal.

Mandatory Multiple Touches Scrimmage

Often a minimum of five touches is prescribed for youth players to develop dribbling and confidence with the ball. One of the best ways to encourage dribbling and discourage mindless kicking of the ball is to demand multiple touches before passing or shooting. The coach can prescribe whatever seems to be appropriate to the day's activity and level of the players. Frequently a minimum of four touches is the prescription. When Weil Coerver introduced this activity during his first visit to the United States in the presence of licensing instructors, former All Americans and other accomplished authorities in soccer all were surprised. None had ever heard of the demand for more touches instead of restricting the number of touches. Here lies the great difference between developing players and developing advanced teams. Many things that we must do to develop youth players are the antithesis of what is done at high levels. The demand for multiple touches engrains mindful control of the ball when no pass is available. It gets away from the mindless kicking of the ball that is often seen in youth games. While parents may be calling "Boot it!", hopefully the youth coach isn't promoting this mindless behavior. At older ages there certainly is a place for 1, 2 and 3 touch activities.

Among the fringe benefits of demanding X number of touches on the ball before releasing it is that players develop fast footwork, gain experience in taking on opponents and find more opportunities for shots. The power of confidence with the ball develops a player of a much higher caliber than those that lack confidence because they can work so much more effectively when playing in tight spaces.

This scrimmage format is often used after the main emphasis of the session was dribbling. Is it hard for the coach to watch a player dribble when there are wide open teammates forward of him? Yes! But there is much more of a problem of mindless kicking of the ball to nowhere in youth soccer. It is also very challenging (frustrating) to the player with poor dribbling skills, but this certainly helps to remedy that problem. As long as the coach ends all sessions with unrestricted play that fosters good decision making in game situations, the temporary effect of the unnatural mandated ball touches is balanced for maximum player development.

Make no mistake; this is a pivotal activity for ages 6-8 and for an even wider age range. Having a couple of neutral players can really help the scrimmage be useful for development and to allow youngsters to have success and fun. This is especially true if the neutrals are among the most accomplished support players on your team.

Defense vs offense

This exercise can be used for dozens of skills, but is outstanding for cover, spreading the offense and for defensive organization. The field is approximately 25 x 40 with a central circle of about 10 yards in diameter. 6v4 is excellent, maybe 5v3 can be effective, but 7v4 or 8v5 with a bigger space is fine. Any numbers of players can be present using the ideal version of 6v4 with frequent substitutions.

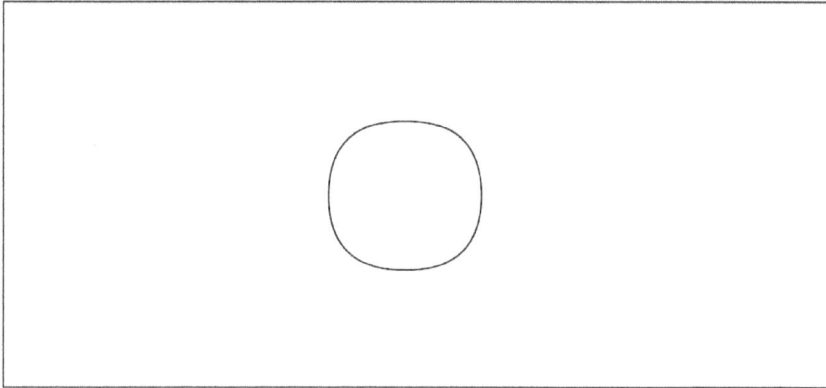

The rules are simple. Two teams: the 6 offensive players attempt to dribble into the center circle and the defenders defend the circle. When the defense wins the ball they simply dribble off the square grid, put their foot on the ball, then take their foot off the ball and count 1001, 1002, 1003. If the offensive players have not taken the ball the defense simply dribble over another side of the grid and score another point. Offense scores by dribbling into the circle, defense by dribbling out of the rectangular grid. Play to a score of 10. Usually on the first occasion the defense wins. No problem, if the offense has not worked out how to use their numbers up, a simple stoppage for questions and clues about spreading out should make the game very competitive. Outstanding activity for ages 10 and older; also occasionally a talented younger team. Excellent all the way to the professional level!

COMBINATION PLAY

The technical details of combination play are seldom clarified, so technical details will be the first area covered for each of the various two man combinations.

Wall Passes: In basic terms the wall pass, 1-2 movement and the give and go are the same. The wall pass is the most familiar and effective method for breaking down a defense when properly executed. Technical details include:
- Eye contact between the two players
- The most overlooked element important to the success is when the player passes the ball to the wall pass receiver, there must be a continuous movement of strong acceleration. The pass and first step are one continuous action. If not executed in this fashion the wall player does not get a chance to see where to pass the ball. The immediate acceleration is absolutely necessary so the wall player can see his teammate's run and then see the ball onto the foot for an accurate one touch return pass. Furthermore, the acceleration allows the player to lose the defender.
- Due to the necessity of excellent accuracy required in the wall pass, both passes require the accurate inside of the foot ground push pass. The return pass must be a lead pass so the player does not have to slow down to receive the ball. At high levels other surfaces must be perfected for long distance implementation.
- The wall player must move to ensure reception, often referred to as showing for the ball, and to create an open path for the return pass. After the pass the wall must also get open for support in case there is a need for another return pass.
- Only repetition will accomplish the timing necessary for success.
- A bent run behind the defender blindsides the opponent and greatly increases the chances of a successful completion
- Generally a one touch wall pass is most effective because the timing is then clear, as opposed to the two touch pass where the receiver doesn't know how much time the wall will use for the return pass. Also the one touch wall pass is much faster, putting more pressure on the defense.

In point of fact, nearly all of the technical elements are accomplished by repetition of the movement. The possible exception is the continuous acceleration by the initial player often requires positive reminders! The distance of wall passes must vary greatly in training as many varied distances are called for in the actual game. At some point, once the wall pass is completed there should be a one touch pass to a third player. The so called third man-on play. This is especially effective if some distance and a change in point of attack is also accomplished. One common fallacy is to only rehearse wall passes vertically (south to north). The wall going across the field is also very important, especially to central midfielders for possession purposes and changes in point of attack.

Naturally the most satisfying wall pass is the one that results in a successful shot on goal. Therefore, wall passes must also be practiced in activities when going to goal. Some such activities follow.

2 Lines facing Each other

This can be used to introduce the technical details of the wall pass. Be sure the two lines are far enough apart for a short dribble, the pass, one touch return pass and room for the pass to the next player in line. A distance of about 20 yards is generally about right. Place cones at that distance as players have a tendency to creep closer and closer together, eliminating quality technical details. This creeping, the destruction of space, is a common problem in many activities. If addressed, demanded consistently even at early ages, player development will be greatly aided. It will save an abundant amount of time for player development for their entire playing career. Even more importantly, it will have carryover to using space appropriately in games!

Right after the demonstration of about ten repetitions, break into two groups if there are 10 or more players. This really is not an activity, it is just a way to teach the technical details and then move on to more game related activities as indicated below.

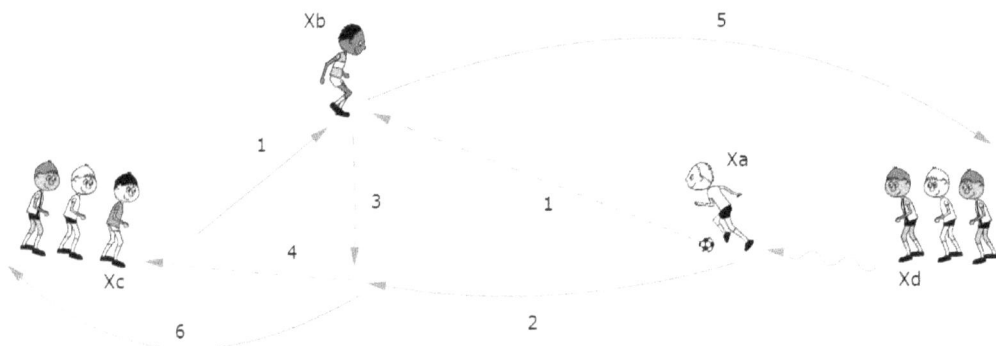

#1 Xb shows for the ball and simultaneously Xa after 1 to 3 touches delivers an accurate moderately crisp pass to Xb, #2 Xa makes a hard run to receive the return pass, #3 the wall pass is made, #4 Xa returns the ball to Xc in the line for another wall pass. #'s 5 & 6 merely show players always sprinting to the end of the opposite line after each trial.

It's actually easier to run the activity in both directions, so now Xd would show for the ball and Xc would pass him the ball, thus wall passes would take place going in both directions. It really is easy if a walk-through is first performed, then a slow version of the activity. Once players have an understanding of the movements, begin to coach the important technical aspects of successful wall passing.

This same format can be used for takeovers, overlaps, quick double passes and one touch passes. This cannot be done for long periods of time, it is only a means of teaching the technical details, then move to wall pass shooting and competitive games clarified in this text.

Repetitive Wall Pass Shots to Goal

This is an activity that is simple and gains a great deal of repetition in a short period of time. Here, players are starting from the midfield circle, allowing enough space for three wall passes before the shot.

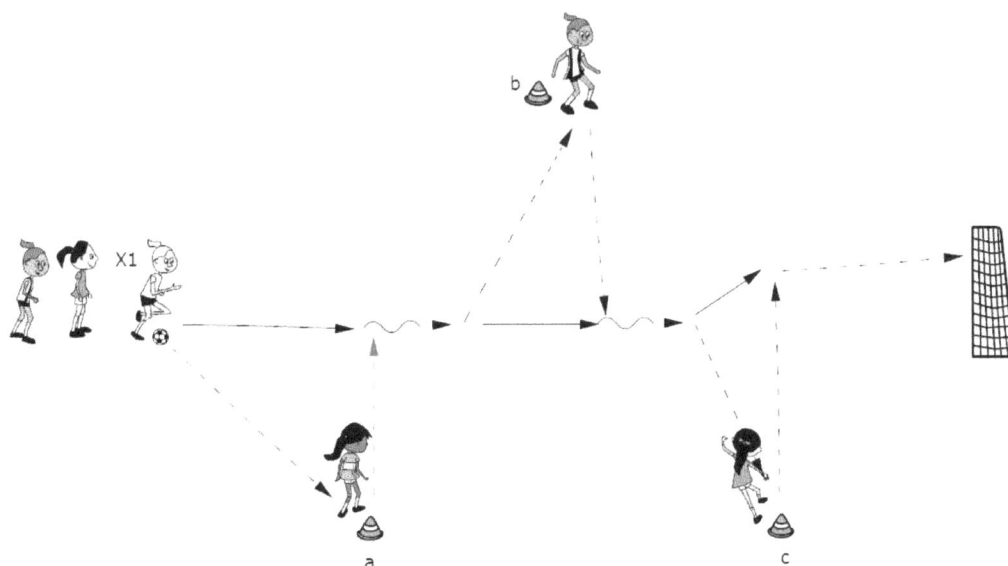

X1 dribbles and plays a wall pass with player at cone a, then repeats the process with player at cones b and c and then shoots on goal. After players can execute the exercise well add a keeper. Probably the second time the activity is used.

Change the players stationed at the cones often and without stopping the exercise. This technique of keeping an activity going while changing roles is to be used often as it leads to improved transition in the game instead of constant stoppages. The more procedures we can do that are game related in training, the better the team will be prepared for games.

1 V 1 with outside Neutrals

The player is required to do a wall pass before going to goal. The error here is that young players will run in front instead of behind the defender. If a player makes the back door run on their own, by all means compliment them. However, this is not an occasion for discovery learning, so correct those that do not go behind the defender, as we do not want to encourage a bad habit.

Attacking player X has dribbled directly at D (defender) and passed to the N (neutral) to his right, ran behind the D and received the return wall pass from N, and scored by dribbling through the cone goal.
Engaging the defender before the pass makes the wall pass more effective.

There is a strong tendency for neutrals to remain stationary. They must be encouraged to move laterally along the line so as to always be in a position to provide support to the attacker. This is a constant problem whenever outside neutrals are used and it requires the coach to establish the habit that neutrals move appropriately. This translates to better movement off the ball in game situations.

Of course, this model employing 1v1 has little change when using the same procedure in shortsided games such as 5v5 or whatever. The only difference might be that the neutral comes onto the field and another player goes outside to perform the neutral role. This translates into mobility in the actual game. Mobility is of great importance to quality soccer. Early introduction simply creates good habits for successful player development.

Alan Maher Continuous Wall Passes Activity

A grid of 20 x 20 yards with players dribbling around the grid and using the "Walls" to execute a give-and-go as shown in the diagram.

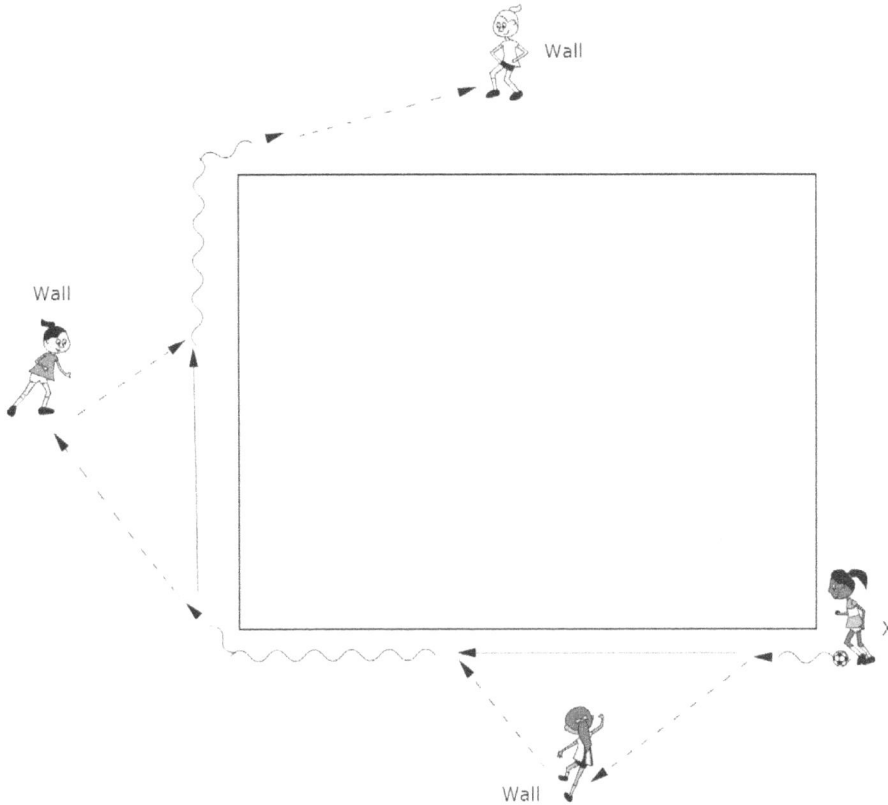

The entire team dribbles around the grid executing wall passes. Be certain players make eye contact, execute accurate passes, and the wall player uses a one touch inside the foot pass. The dribbler needs to accelerate with the passing touch sent to the wall player.

The wall players must step to the ball for every pass and then back well away from the grid to make space for the next wall pass. **"Use space, make space"** needs to be incorporated into all exercises. Of course sometimes it is the reverse, **"Make space, use space"**. Essentially that is checking away and then to the ball. Encouraging game-like movement in all exercises will pay big dividends in players long range development. If necessary place a cone to postion the wall players.

Since the rest of the team is also dribbling around, players need to use timing and vision to keep the exercise moving smoothly. Change the wall players every few minutes. With a shortage of players simply reduce the number of wall players.

In this exercise it is best to focus on corrections and rewards with individuals, although if a coaching point pertains to all players by all means make a coaching stoppage. Be certain to reverse the direction from clockwise to counter-clockwise half way through the exercise.

Move to an induced wall pass game. Possibly require two wall passes before going to goal. If you see an east-west wall pass, by all means show its value to the whole team. Be certain to end the session with unrestricted play and hope you see a wall pass being made. If that happens without your demanding it you likely have had a very good session!

Group of the Whole

One ball for every 3 or 4 players can have players randomly performing wall passes in a large grid. Be sure all players are moving to all areas of the grid and performing wall passes with many different members of the team.

The problem that arises is that a player plays a wall pass, gets the return pass and doesn't know how **not** to be the one with the ball all the time. Here is how it is done in the exercise and in the game. When a player passes the ball and does not want it returned, just turn away **immediately** after the pass, eyes and body. Also the run is away from the wall player. The immediacy is necessary so the receiver sees you do not want a return pass. This is obviously the opposite of when a player wants the ball back because in that case he makes eye contact. This is clearly a form of visual communication. Not all communication is verbal. There are many reasons a player in a game may not want a return pass such as exhaustion, being over-matched by her defender, seeing better opportunities for the receiver in forward positions, etc.

So much is said about the verbal communication, but seldom is there adequate instruction in hand signals, runs and eye communication. Body position is also a form of communication. The beauty of these non-verbal communications is that often they are hidden from the defender!

ADVANCED LEVEL
Team Games Doing the Wall Pass

This is more for ages 10 and above. Both teams have their own ball in the same area and perform wall passes. Move to doing a wall pass to any intervening player. Progress to one ball and doing a wall pass to an opposing player. Score a point for each successful completion. Keep score. You can mix and match some of these activities such as any wall pass counts 1 point and any wall pass done to the opposing team member counts 5 points. The final scrimmage can be one point for all wall passes, two points for a wall pass with an intervening opponent and five points for a wall pass that results in a goal. **Note how methods of scoring can greatly enhance whatever the coach wants the players to learn.**

Advanced coaches often start scrimmages with artificial scores to reinforce their objectives. For instance, a coach who wants players to play more possession when ahead and take more risks when losing in a game might start the X team with a score of 2-0. Thus the Y teams might play more direct, take many chances and the X team would be encouraged to possess the ball more. If the coach wanted the whole team to exhibit both behaviors more effectively, just reverse the score assignments every 8 minutes. Simply manipulate scores to facilitate what you want players to learn to do!

#1 Xa and Xb have made eye contact, Xb shows for the ball; #2 Xa delivers a skip pass to Xb,(skip pass means that it goes past teammate Xc); #3 Xa makes a hard run behind defender Ya; #4 Xb delivers a one touch lead wall pass to Xa and play continues.

Takeovers are very powerful when the technical details are properly executed. Technical details are:

- When the ball is taken from a teammate, the ball is knocked several yards accompanied by outstanding acceleration to stay with the ball.
- The takeover is never a short pass as this would permit the defenders of both players to double-team the receiver.
- The dribbling player has the ball moving at a very slow pace, or may even stop the ball by placing her foot on top of the ball. However, the player giving up the ball is always with the ball until it is taken over by a teammate. One reason this is done is that on occasion the takeover is a decoy move: instead of the takeover, the original player plucks the ball away from the on-coming teammate and keeps the ball herself (this actually is the most deceiving functional technique of the takeover). When this is done the player invariably loses her marker.
- The signal for a takeover is when a teammate is under so much pressure that she cannot get her head up to look for a pass, so a teammate 'saves her' by going at speed and takes the ball away.
- Takeovers are done left to left and right to right so that the ball is always shielded from the defender(s) and there is a smooth movement devoid of collisions.
- There is a very advanced takeover move in which a dribbling player is going forward, and a teammate going at great speed crosses in front and takes the ball, leaving both markers behind the new ball carrier. See diagram. More for higher level teams.

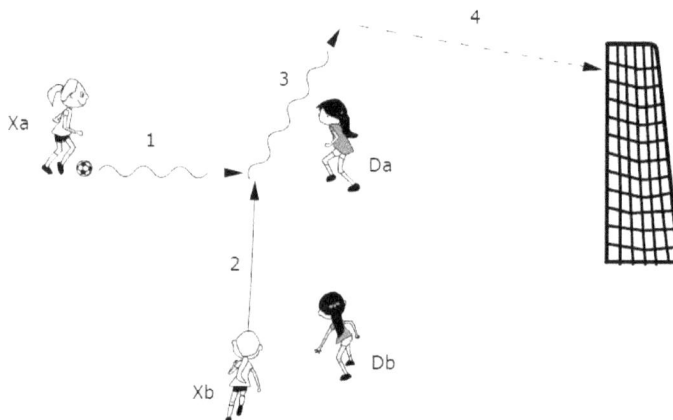

#1 Xa is dribbling forward and marked by Da; #2 Xb comes at speed and takes the ball, hopefully leaving both defenders behind; #3 Xb is free of both defenders. #4 Xb fires a shot on goal. This diagonally forward crisscross movement can even confuse sophisticated defenses.

This is a very exciting play that when done in the penalty area creates havoc for a defense.

It is good to keep in mind that takeovers can be done in any direction anywhere on the field. Doing takeovers east/west near the 18 yard line can end with a shot on goal. This certainly helps players realize its usefulness, especially after they can do it well technically with the inclusion of the plucking for a fake takeover with a shot on goal. This takeover can be done with a single defender. This is more of an age 10 and beyond activity.

The ultimate teaching of the takeover might be the takeover followed by a mini square run, or "spinout", by the player who gave up the ball and a diagonal return pass to his teammate that results in a shot on goal. The reason for the square run spinout is to maintain an on-sides position.

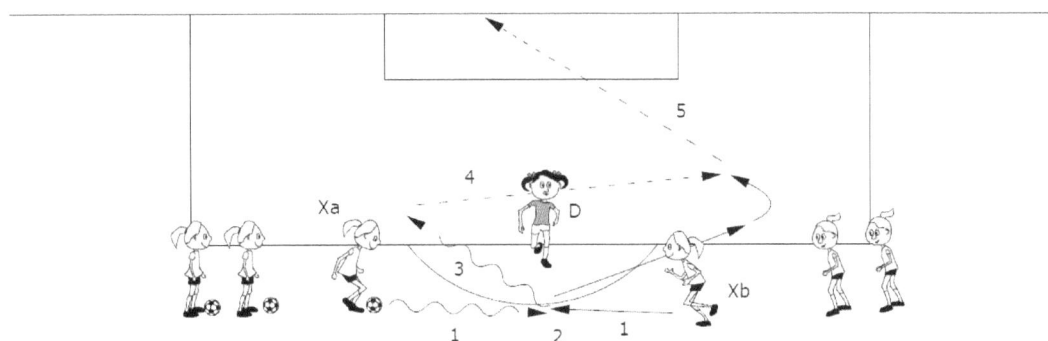

#1 Xa dribbles toward Xb: simultaneously Xb moves toward Xa; #2 is the takeover (in this case to shield the ball from the defender that is goal side the players are both using their right foot); #3 Xb now has the ball, dribbles diagonally forward; #4 Xb passes with the left foot to Xa: #5 Xa takes a shot on goal. This move of running square and turning away from the goal then going forward to receive the return pass is often referred to as a 'Spinout'.

Start with no defender, move to defender with hands behind the back, then to active defender. With the active defender all movements are permitted; plucking, the actual takeover, and/or the spinout option.

The exercise continues with the next two players. After each trial the players go to the opposite line. On the second or third occasion of the exercise, reverse the direction so that now we have a left to left takeover and the pass is made with the right foot.

After you realize the various options associated with the takeover, fake takeover (plucking) and the spinout, you begin to realize the confusion the takeover can inflict on a defense. The main problem is getting players to make a nearly square pass (actually it is a slight diagonal forward pass). Players always seem to want to make a forward pass that really becomes a pass to the opposing keeper, thus destroying the value of the exercise. Once you begin the induced scrimmage, give one point for every takeover, allow 3 points for goals that result from a takeover, and 6 points for goals that result from a spinout takeover. This is not likely to happen on the first 2 or 3 times you do takeovers in a scrimmage format. When it happens both the coach and players will definitely celebrate, and rightly so!

The Overlap seems to be often trained for but seldom executed in game situations, except at the highest levels. Maybe this is so because youth teams, high school and college teams lack mobility to begin with. There is a strong tendency for most defenders to stay back and play safely, which is understandable since we often choose them to be defenders because they have a good understanding of safety. Now all of a sudden we want them to attack. This requires considerable coaching encouragement to go forward and execute an overlap. Midfielders are probably a little less reluctant to stay back, and maybe a bit easier to encourage to go forward, serve crosses and take shots on goal. In any case the overlap is a very important and valuable attacking tactic.

Admittedly with 5-8 aside there are not four defenders, so without players filling in for the defenders the reluctance is even greater. Also, we all know how hard it is when the team is attacking to get a youth player to fall back. In any case we must introduce and encourage all the two man tactics early on, even at ages 7-11. Once players begin to think of a position, instead of team shape, they start to think that there is a specific place on the field to position oneself. They may think that they have a certain relative place they must stay at in relation to their teammates. Players in programs that lack mobility from ages 5-12 are often somewhat damaged. Actually, the beauty of 3-a-side is that there are no positions.

Overlaps are of numerous varieties. Many are mentioned here. It also is one of the best ways to teach players how to create space for a teammate. This is a difficult problem for a young player to learn, but the overlap greatly simplifies the process as it allows the coach to show simple worthwhile movements that teach the player how to make space for a teammate. We will deal with the simplest and most common overlap first to clarify the technical aspects of the move.

The most common overlap is an outside defender moving forward to a serving/striking location. A ball passed to an outside midfielder often initiates the movement. The overlap has excellent chances for success when the outside midfielder knows how to create space on the flank. This usually means a square or slightly diagonal dribble to the inside of the field that opens up space on the flank as shown in the diagram.

Technical details of the overlap are:

- A very fast run by the wingback near the touchline. The hard run is necessary so that he is not behind a defender for any length of time, and thus unavailable as a receiver. This would make the defending team's job easy since the receiver would not have outside support. Players near the ball must be open for the maximum amount of time during the overlap, which is what the hard sprint provides.
- The inside dribble by the player (often the outside midfielder) dribbling inside creates space on the flank for the outside overlap----this is made extremely clear in the diagram.
- Feinting a pass or any action that makes the defense think the ball is going inside to a dangerous shooting location in the middle of the field also opens up the flank. This naturally requires that central players work hard to get free to increase the fear of the inside pass, which in some cases will actually happen. Thus the overlap created opportunities in the central area of the field as well as the flank.
- Defenders cannot, and generally will not, go forward unless teammates fill in the vacated location. This is especially true in the defending half of the field. However, such overlaps are rare and do not occur unless time is running out and the team is desperate due to being behind in the score. When in the attacking half, filling in at the back is not as necessary, and is in fact contrary to the overlap, as the overlap is attempting to get numbers up in specific locations in the attacking half.
- Generally the overlapper becomes a server, thus it behooves teammates to fill the goal area slots to be receivers of the overlapper's service. Slots are near-post about two yards forward of the post and two yards from the endline. The near post occupation is mainly to deny the keeper the ball. Second slot is 4 or 5 yards back from the far post and 6 or 7 yards from the goal line. Both locations vary widely due to the offside law. The third slot is somewhere just outside the penalty spot.

Diagram of outside wingback overlap:

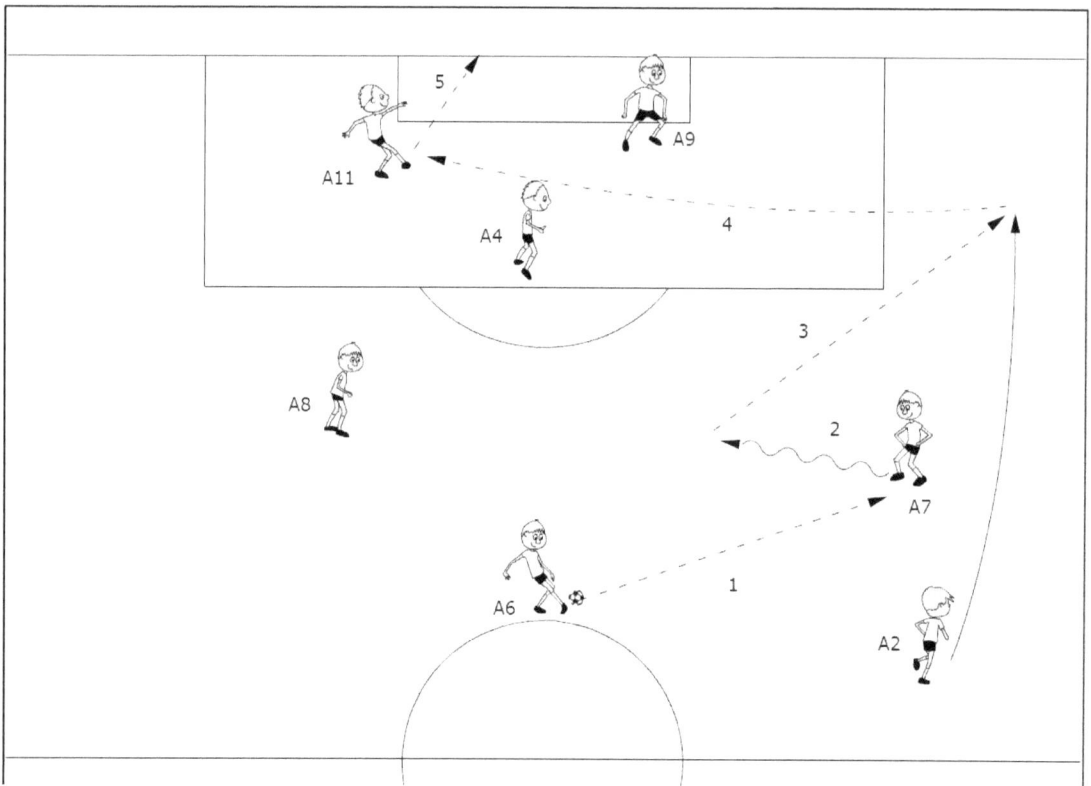

#1) A6 has passed the ball to outside midfielder A7: #2) A7 the outside midfielder dribbles inside making space for overlapping player A2   #3) A7 passes to the flank to A2 who has sprinted forward and receives a pass on the vacated flank: #4) A2, the overlapper delivers service to the goal area #5) A11 takes the shot. Note A9, A11 & A4 attackers have filled the slots.

The key to the entire movement is the inside dribble which makes space on the flank. If the dribble is only a yard or two it is unlikely to create adequate flank space. A distance of 5 to 10 yards or more is likely to be adequate.

Overlaps that go across the field (so called east/west) can help create rapid changes in attack and therefore create problems to the defense. Mini overlaps inside the penalty area create chaos because in this area enormous attention is given to the ball. So when a teammate crosses the ball carrier with a square run she is often left free. Dennis Berkamp, the famous Dutch striker, was notorious for this movement and scored goals from it at the highest levels of the game.

The Inside Overlap is nothing more than a player (generally a striker) somewhat centrally located going out to the flank for a pass that she must run onto, receive and often serve a cross.

Many coaches do much more with pattern play, but it may be best just to introduce the two man combinations at an early age and as players mature they will become more and more adept at their appropriate usage. Once they become competent in the technical aspects of combination play their usage will be a result of the game situation demands as opposed to patterns. At high levels patterns are employed, but are much less appropriate for young players. It is hard to understand the passion for creative playing and high usage of rigid patterns that may never present themselves in game situations. However, such very generalized patterns such as inside/out and outside/in, that encourage hips facing teammates, permit vision, and foster quick changes in point of attack are extremely productive.

Most of all pattern play is for upper levels of the game because they consume a great deal of time and they deny players touches of the ball. Furthermore, youth teams that practice only one or two times a week cannot waste precious time on patterns that involve sedentary situations.

Having players knowledgeable of the technical details of combination play with adequate repetition starting at an early age will allow them to find game situations for their productive usage. This technical repetition of the combinations will greatly foster player creativity that seems to be so often criticized. Criticizing is easy, but have we trained the players adequately for mobility to foster their creativity?

Mobility is tied to combination play because combinations require that a player leave his position. Overlaps by definition mean leaving one's position. Wall passes and takeovers also require leaving one's position.

The final area that makes combinations extremely powerful in game situations is when immediately following the combination play, a one touch pass, a quick shot of significant distance and/or a change in the direction of play occurs. This is referred to as the third man-on. This is so powerful and exciting that even lay soccer spectators ooh and ah when it occurs! This was very noticeable at World Cup 1994 USA. The American spectators, at that point still somewhat unsophisticated, recognized the beauty of combination play with a third man on, as evidenced by the audible roars from the crowd.

DEFENSE

The three main principles of defense are **PRESSURE**, **COVER** and **BALANCE**. Only pressure and cover are a concern for young players. Balance even at ages beyond 12 is often only average or below. If the youth coach can teach basic pressure and cover he will have been very successful. Cover in particular is generally very weak, often due to the fact that many coaches over-emphasize marking, and yet marking in most cases is only to be imposed AFTER PRESSURE AND COVER IS ESTABLISHED! Of course, in the immediate goal area marking is mandatory. In this case the keeper is often the cover player.

Pressure is fairly simple. The player closest to the ball gets right in front of the opponent with the ball. Generally within a yard distance, feet shoulder width apart, knees bent, and hands out for balance with eye on the ball. At upper levels, 11 aside soccer, a line of defense is established by the coach, but this is not a concern for ages 4-11. Line of defense is merely the location at which a team will apply consistent pressure on the ball. This can vary widely, but with equally matched teams it most frequently is applied somewhere in the opponent's half of the field.

Pressure tries to make it hard for the player with the ball to move it forward by dribbling or passing. Naturally it tries to deny the opponent from shooting. The biggest issue with pressure is that it must be applied early, as quickly as possible. There must be a great urgency to get to the opponent with the ball quickly. A few quick steps or even a sprint is often necessary. However, when the defender gets near the ball she must slow down and get into the boxer stance, and if the opportunity avails itself win the ball. Winning the ball is not the priority until the pressure player has cover. Once the pressure player has cover, winning the ball takes on a much more assertive posture. Until cover is established the player is mostly concerned with delay; denying penetration. Double teaming is not recommended except if a third player is providing cover. Usually young players naturally play double teaming too often as they always want the ball.

Regan for a young player is showing good defensive stance. Knees bent, feet could be a bit wider, back reasonably straight, hands out for balance and to force the attacking player to go around them, and eye on the ball.

One of the main problems with youth players is that they kick at the ball instead of tackling. Techniques for tackling are exactly like the push pass position except the player is much lower in a more powerful body position. Inside of the foot to the ball, leaning forward slightly on balls of the feet, shoulder into the opponent and possibly moving the ball to the easiest location to control the ball. That place for a right footed player doing a right footed tackle is usually to the left. If the ball is loose for a moment maybe a chop of the ball to the left is in order. Unfortunately, excellent tacklers of the ball are not so technical as they are very determined, tenacious and confident of winning the ball. Success is more dependent on a mental set than on technique, though technique is still a factor.

Two young tacklers are doing well by having toes up, being low, leaning into opponent, knees bent and arms out. Probably they could have gotten their shoulders into the opponent a bit better.

Cover is a whole different situation. Establishing the correct distance and angle is important. That usually means about 2 to 5 yards depending on one's speed, the opponent's speed and skill, and the field location. For mature players it is further. It is always a distance that will not allow the ball carrier to beat the pressure player and then have another 1v1 situation with the cover player. When the attacker touches the ball past the pressure player the cover player must always be able to get the ball before the attacker.

The angle means seeing the ball and the most dangerous offensive support player, then placing oneself a bit toward that player. In the vicinity of the goal it means goal side. Cover also means communicating to the pressure player with such commands as "You got cover", "Tackle the ball", "Steer right" or any information that will help deny penetration and win the ball. As the players get

127

older the quality of communication will improve. But it is important that we start them talking to help the pressure player at an early age.

The **Klivecka Activity** in the Shortsided Games section is outstanding for instructing both offensive support and defensive cover.

As indicated earlier, cover is a critical skill and possibly one that USA players are a bit weaker at than in countries that have soccer as their main sport. In those countries young players see much more high level professional soccer and intuitively some of the vision of cover is absorbed at an earlier age. Also, the previously mentioned obsession with marking sets the seeds for a problem.

In all fairness there is also an indigenous problem. In 2v2 and even 3 through 5 aside, early marking is very critical because often the opponent is in shooting distance of the goal because of the small field. Also, no goalkeeper causes fewer players available for cover which forces concerted marking. Another factor is that 1v1 is a critical training environment that should be used abundantly with young players, in which case marking is built right into the environment and there is no cover player in 1v1. In spite of all this, players need to be well trained and somewhat competent with cover by age 11. If they are not, they will have already formed a bad habit of not covering and this habit is extremely difficult to break at ages 13-18.

Certainly there is no major fault in spending a few minutes on defensive organization, but already the win mania likely spends too much time on team organization of defense. Thus it is not covered to any great extent in this text. Of course at high levels defensive organization is critical.

If offensive skills such as dribbling, controlled passing/receiving, collecting and all manner of ball control skills are not well established, there is little need for defense since players will turn the ball over by themselves.

This is why all offensive skills must be established before defensive skills get much attention. We all know why inappropriate defensive emphasis is instructed a great deal before it should be----that is the desire to win a U-5 through U-12 game as though it was a World Cup final. Granted it is difficult to maintain focus on player development in an exciting game such as soccer. Nonetheless, adult maturity is demanded for coaches of young players in sports just as with any other youth activity. No one would consider short cuts for mountain climbing, sky diving, bungee jumping, etc. Maybe not even in swimming, skiing or shooting target practice. Keeping one's perspective on player development pays huge dividends in the long term!

Suffice it to say the deep sweeper often played at ages 7-11, and often well beyond, is a disaster. It is a very bad habit that succeeds because many coaches do not know how to beat it, but a knowledgeable coach with some preparation will destroy this arrangement. This is not a theory, but in fact I have experienced this often. Simply attack down one flank, usually very easy to do, draw the sweeper, and send the ball to the weak side. This tactic destroys even the more astute young sweepers.

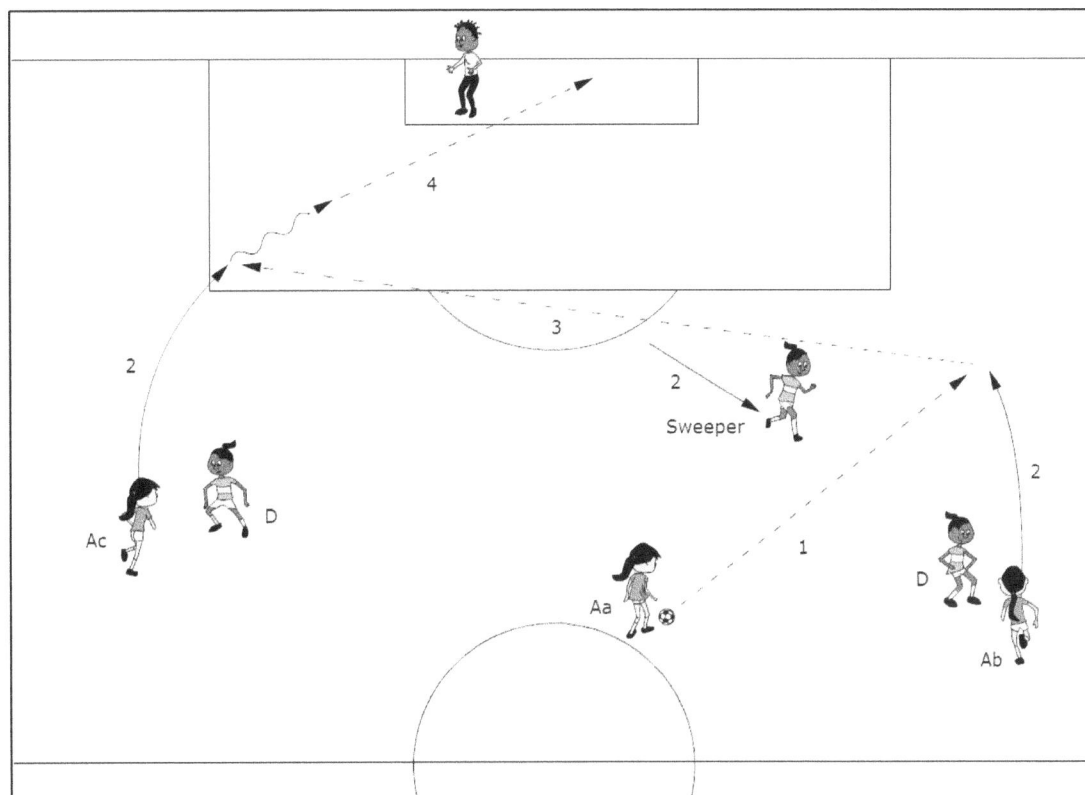

A = Attacking team: #1 In this case a central player Aa has played the ball to the outside right of the field, to Ab #2 Ab has run behind the right side defender to receive and is on-sides due to the deep sweeper, also Ac was on-sides #3 Ab sends a long diagonal ball to the far side to Ac, #4 Ac is now 1v1 with the keeper for shot on goal.

There are numerous ways to draw the sweeper to one side of the field; dribbling and/or passing and then a big change in point of attack to an on-sides teammate on the far side of the field. Instead of an offsides trap denying the attack in these situations, it often facilitates an on-sides attack.

Thus, there are no sweepers any longer at high levels of play. Using tactics that are ineffective and incorrect to win games while establishing bad habits is contrary to player development. This kind of youth soccer distorts long range player development. Unfortunately this is all too common.

What is always imperative for good soccer and to develop good early habits, is that the team move as a unit. On offense, spread out and move up the field, on defense compact and put pressure and cover on the ball. More mature teams also must be competent with defensive balance.

The briefness of the defensive coverage is in line with the premise set forth earlier to establish ball control, dribbling, basic passing skills, and combination play first and foremost. After that is accomplished, more attention can be given to defense. Also, defense is not as much technical as it is fitness oriented. Good defenders have ability to run at pace and a strong mentality. They take pride in not getting beat and denying goal scoring!

SHOOTING

These exercises cover the entire range of shooting for youngsters ages 4-12. The most important thing to take away from this chapter is do a lot of shooting because players love to shoot! At the end of a game the score indicates which team scored the most goals. Quality passing/receiving and combination play will create the opportunities for shots on goal.

Whenever activities at practice are dragging a little, insert a shooting activity and watch the interest level get totally revived! Jimmy Lennox, an icon of U.S. soccer at collegiate level, but even more importantly as the former director of the National Soccer Coaches of America licensing schools said, "Shooting at goal must be incorporated into every training session!". This might be even more important for youth teams than it is for high level teams.

Shooting activities for youth are:

Circle Shooting

This is an excellent exercise because there is a lot of repetition and it is so simple that even the youngest players can do it with a minimum of instruction. Simply have one able youngster show the circular pattern and then the rest just follow. The setup is as shown.

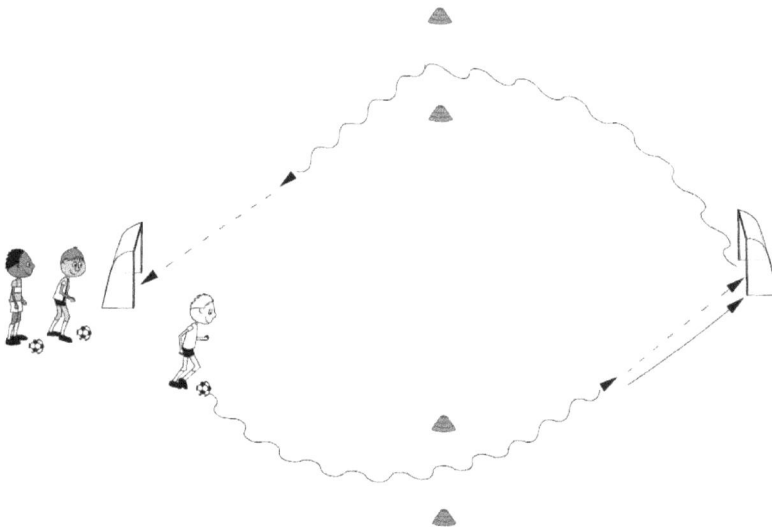

Each player has his own ball and simply dribbles through the gate goal and shoots at one goal and then the other in a circular fashion. As players get older the gate should be wider with a line defender with hands behind his back. Eventually have a line defender unrestricted.

The small goals should be about 30 yards apart. Players retrieve their own balls. Once players have done the exercise 1 or 2 times demand a shot be taken behind a cone or vest the appropriate distance away from the goal. For the very youngest about 5 yards away, and for older groups considerably further away. Progressively increase the distance as the players' competence increases. Be certain to provide some time going in the opposite direction (clockwise), thus facilitating use of the left foot. Keep it moving, tell youngsters to just go ahead of the player in front of them if the player in front needs time to retrieve his ball, or for any other reason. Give individual coaching points to players. Finer coaching points can be added on subsequent occasions, such as speed dribble through the gate. Shoot toward the far inside netting. After 2 or 3 occasions encourage the shot on the first touch after going through the gate. Place the gate at the appropriate distance. Definitely insist on low shots, so-called worm burners. We have all seen so many wasted opportunities fly over the goal post! For older groups, with full sized age appropriate goals, a keeper can be added.

Pairs setting up teammate for a shot

Two players dribble and pass in the large area doing two touches, but not the smaller area of 12 x 30. Adjust dimensions to the level of your players. The pairs are numbered one through whatever number of pairs there are. When you call out "One", the member of that pair who has the ball must pass it to his partner for a one touch shot. If the partner really doesn't have a one touch shot he passes it back to his partner for a one touch shot. Demand movement with and without the ball! Call out the pairs in random order after the first round.

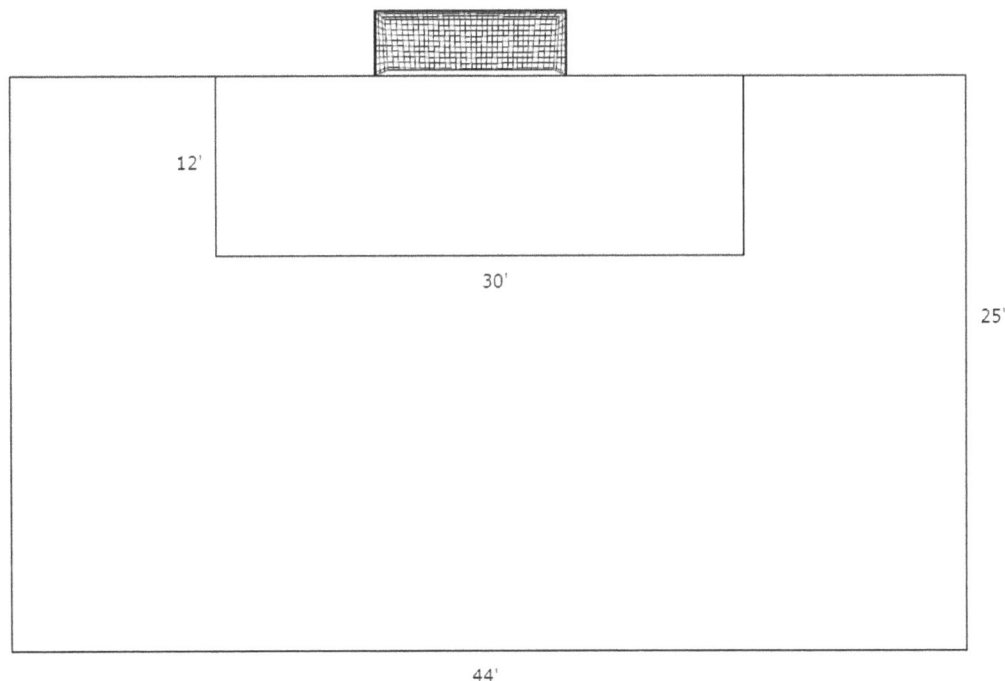

The no entry area is 12 x 30 yards, with the passing/receiving area being 25 x 44 yards. You can use any dimensions appropriate to the ability level of your players.

This is a great activity as it teaches assisting in the goal area, getting to a useful location ahead of time for a one touch shot, increases vision, fosters proper body position (both eye contact and trying to face the goal for a shot), and of course taking the one touch shot.

Demand that close-in shots be accurate placed balls as opposed to power shots. Besides safety, passing shots are much quicker because power shots require a longer period of preparation! This time delay causes many shots to never be executed. Of course, shots taken from distance require power instep drives.

This was the second time this group did this exercise and as a result they were doing an excellent job positioning themselves facing the goal when they were without the ball. They also managed to have good spacing between the pair and in relation to the other pairs. Wow!

Jeff Pill Shooting

This activity involves enormous repetition, competition and movement. Simply set up two flags about 6 yards apart (varies with age/ability) and have balanced pairs of players as a team.

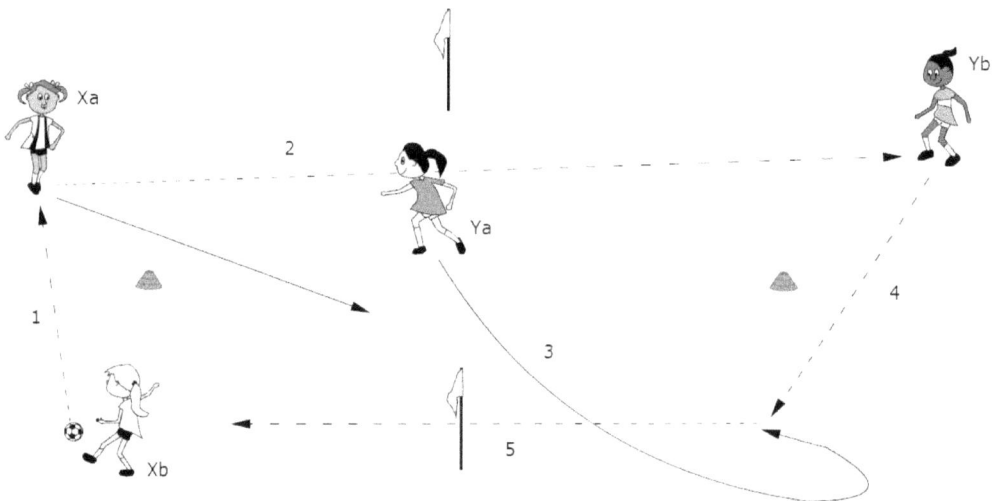

#1 Xb has the ball and lays it off to Xa for a demanded one touch shot; #2 Xa attempts to score below head height of Ya who is defending the goal; #3 if Xa scores Ya runs back to receive the ball from Yb; #4 after Yb collects the ball she passes to Ya #5 Ya shoots to score for her team at the same time one of the X players has moved into the flag goal to defend.

Encourage all ball contacts to be one touch. If the shot is saved the ball is given to a teammate and again a shot is attempted. Rapid transition is an integral part of this shooting activity.

All shots are one touch and taken from behind the cones, as indicated in the diagram. This is a very fast paced exciting functional game. The ball should never stop moving! If the ball does stop the opponents are awarded a point. Layoffs, square passes and through pass shots are all employed. At the first opportunity for a shot, the shot must be taken. In many instances this means a single touch from one partner resulting in a shot by the other partner. Naturally the team that scores the most goals wins. The collateral learning is that players often learn to follow their shot in order to get ready for the opponent's shot as quickly as possible.

Option: Players stay back and each touches the ball once and sends the ball back through the flags without anyone becoming a goalkeeper.

Goal Line Numbers

Two teams are formed each on different sides of the goal, behind the goal line. Each team has a player designated #1, #2, #3, etc. The coach is also on the goal line with all the balls. The coach calls out a number and serves out a ball about 15 to 20 yards out from the goal line. That pair competes for the ball and the one who gets the ball tries to score and the other defends. Later on call out two or three numbers for 2v2 or 3v3. End the shooting activity by sending a ball about 25 yards from goal and call out, "Everyone". Now it is a whole team shooting activity.

Try to always be certain that whenever a scoring opportunity in a game type activity occurs, players shoot. If this is done consistently, players will not be passing up goal scoring opportunities in actual games.

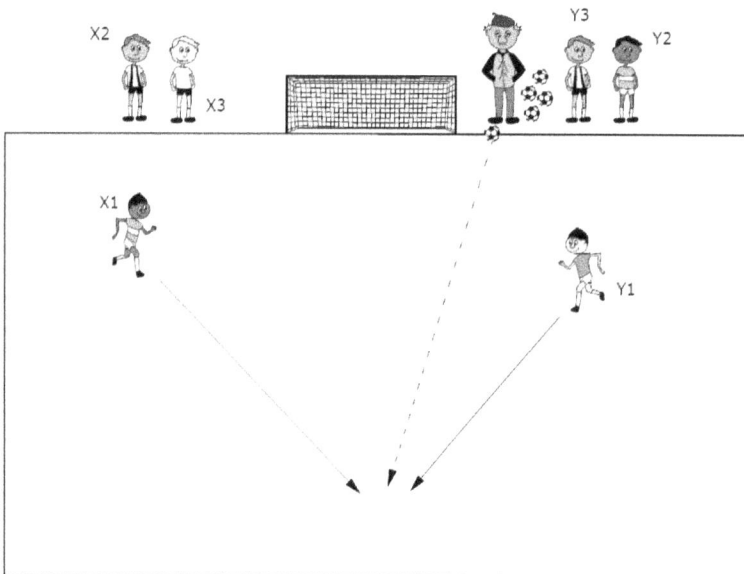

The coach has all the balls. Call out a second pair after a player from the previous pair has control of the ball.

Why the phase "Be more selfish" evolved is confusing and likely incorrect. Most available shots that are not executed are a result of lack of confidence and fear of failure. It is selfish to pass responsibility to another player when an opportunity occurs. Be less selfish, shoot when quality opportunities occur!

Keep this activity moving along quickly. Even with 10 or 12 players I find that this involves a great deal of fitness due to the rigor of 1v1. Require players to keep a team score.

Goal Box Chaos

Goal Box Chaos, sometimes called 'Bull Pen', has two teams on a very short field, about 25 yards, with full field width and two goals. Players must shoot at every opportunity. Each team has a keeper who distributes a ground ball to a teammate whenever he makes a save.

One point for a shot on goal, three points for a goal, one point deducted by the coach every time a player has a shot and does not shoot.

The coach can encourage layoffs and combinations that would create a shot. To increase the chances for shots, add one or two neutral players to help the team in possession. This activity is also great for achieving defensive transition.

Option: have two wide players in a channel serving crosses. There can be only one player on each side serving to whichever team gave him the ball. Switch servers often. With more mature level teams every time the player serves he moves onto the field and a teammate assumes the role of server.

Besides players loving this exercise and thus making great effort, there is a major need to do exercises of this type if we are going to expect players to have some composure in the goal area when playing actual matches!

More Shooting: All the 1v1 games played to regulation goals for the age are possibilities, especially the Spots Game, Holohan Shooting and Barnello Fitness Shooting, all in the 1v1 section. "Repetitive Wall Pass Shots to Goal" and "1v1 with Outside Neutrals" shown in the combination play section are also excellent.

Don't expect good shooting technique and decisions if you are not spending adequate amounts of time on shooting and finishing. Not only is it a very important skill, but it is also fun for players, which increases their general motivation.

HEADING

This clearly is a minor skill for ages 4-7, but that does not mean it is not introduced. For ages 4-6 it is often enough to just have the players hold the ball and touch it to their forehead, leaving their eyes open and the head tilted way back. Actually, when heading the eyes blink when the ball contacts the head, but what we are teaching here is to keep the eyes open until the ball makes contact with the forehead. Also we are setting the proper location of the ball contact in a non-threatening manner.

The key is to do very simple low level activities that build confidence for heading over a long period of time. A reduced inflation of the ball helps a great deal. Also quality balls that are not hard or heavy are a necessity. Developing neck muscles by having players gently with their hands resist a teammate's movement of the head in all four directions will greatly help players develop neck strength for heading skills. When a player attacks the ball and neck muscles can keep the head steady, heading is comfortable.

A common fault is contacting the ball with the top of the head, which is incorrect and potentially dangerous. The skull bone in the head is not fused until about age 20! A further progression is self service, having a player toss the ball about two feet in the air, head it up and catch it. Next players can self toss the ball to a higher height. Most will toss the ball an appropriate height in accordance with their courage, confidence and ability.

Later on, at about age seven, progress to pairs, one sitting and the other lobbing the ball USING A TWO HAND UNDERHAND TOSS from about 5 feet, which would place the 'tosser' about three feet away from the sitting player's feet. Too close is not an advantage as it does not allow the heading player time to adjust to the toss. Switch roles regularly. Never do an entire session of heading. Instead, heading progressions are done for 5-10 minutes in successive sessions. The full progression occurs all the way to age 12, but still less than 15 minute segments.

The next step is often heading from a kneeling position with increasing use of the abdominal muscles for future power heading. Arms should move to propel the player forward with some authority. Progress to standing which should be fine about age 8 or 9.

Threes in a triangle shape is excellent so that player #1 tosses the ball to player #2 who heads the ball to player #3. The focus of threes is to get players to be able to change the direction of the ball. Have players head the ball down to the feet of player #3. This is a good situation to get some collecting skill accomplished along with the heading. Instead of the third player catching the ball, have him collect the ball and then pick it up.

In time have 3 players working together with a player between the tosser and the player heading the ball. Eventually the heading player is required to jump to head the ball. At some point have players head the ball to a goal attempting to direct the ball downward toward the goal line to an open area.

Proper location on forehead

With ages 4 & 5 this simple activity introduces the proper location on the forehead for heading a soccer ball. Also by extending the neck fully backward a bit of neck strength is developed. This could be sufficient for this age level---groups that show readiness for more can self serve the ball up about 2-3 feet and head the ball and then catch the ball.

Pairs in friendly underhand service: Note the heading player is sitting in an attempt to get players to use abdominal muscles and their hands.

Players in a line heading: First Xa serves to Xb who returns the ball to Xa ; then Xc serves to Xb. Clearly the main benefit of this exercise is many repetitions in a very short period of time.

Three players in a triangle configuration are juggling with emphasis on heading to the third player: Excellent for changing direction of ball using the heading skill.

Heading the ball down to the goal line. By introducing the goal, effort is immediately increased. The emphasis here is on getting the head above the ball and heading the ball down to the goal line completely negating the keepers use of the hands.

Diving Headers to Goal: While this is somewhat of a novelty activity, players seem to enjoy the challenge and thus makes it worthwhile. The rest of the team was with the other coach in order to have as little time as possible of inactivity. This 8 year old made a strong full dive.

For ages 9 and above all the way to high school level there is a very exciting heading game. Players merely set up 4 cones, 2 for each goal line as shown. Goal line width is about 2 yards with the distance between the goals being about 5 yards. Two pairs of players compete in heading the ball over the opposing goal line defended by the 2 opponents on the goal line who cannot use their hands. Goals cannot be higher than the defenders' heads.

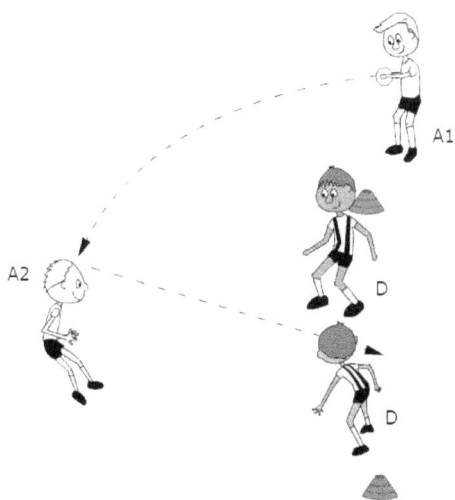

A1 serves a two handed underhand serve from behind the opponents for his teammate to head at the two defending opponents; defenders are on their goal line. The entire game is played by whoever retrieves the ball first, it's their ball!

143

Viehwager Heading: Hard to believe these U-12 year olds head with such authority. Due to the fast movement in this game players request its use---imagine young girls requesting a heading game, and you begin to realize how great a game this really is!

Servers always run behind the opponent's goal line to serve to their teammates. That gives them the best chance to score because the distance gives their teammate power to attack the ball. If a team has a hand ball while defending the opponent's header the attackers get a penalty header, meaning the opponents must put an ear on each cone and their feet protecting the goal line.

Viehwager Heading Penalty Shot: Momo just scored this goal below knee height between the defending players legs. When you realize that the ball bounced up in the air this far away you begin to realize the power of this header! Games achieve levels of skill development that cannot be achieved by drills!

Now the shooter, the player heading the ball, must score below knee height since the opponents are lying on the ground. Players will develop advanced strategies such as while one player is retrieving the ball the other will go behind the opponent's goal line, receive a pass and serve to the quick moving forward teammate who retrieved the ball. Every five minutes change opponents, winners against winners.

Generally it is best to set this up while the group is busy doing another exercise or getting a water break. Pull an able group for the demonstration of the game. In this manner you will have worked out the kinks of the game and your demo players will be able to provide a very clear demonstration of the game with no waste of time or loss of the group's attention. This is a good technique to use often. Groups can set up their own cones once they have seen the demonstration group's setup. The time saved by having more than one coach, no matter how capable the coach, is enormous over the course of a whole season. More repetition, more fun, all of which results in a better program. If the demonstration group was setting up while the team was getting a drink break, after the demonstration have them take their water break.

Just listen to the joyous sounds made by players when engaged in this game! While post session self assessment of your coaching is a good habit, the joyous sounds of players in developmental skill games such as this are a better indicator. It's incredible how well players who are reluctant to head the ball are suddenly attacking the ball with confidence because they are engaged in a worthwhile and fun skill development game.

Wambach Heading

Wambach Heading has four players with two servers and the other two competing to head the ball back to the server.

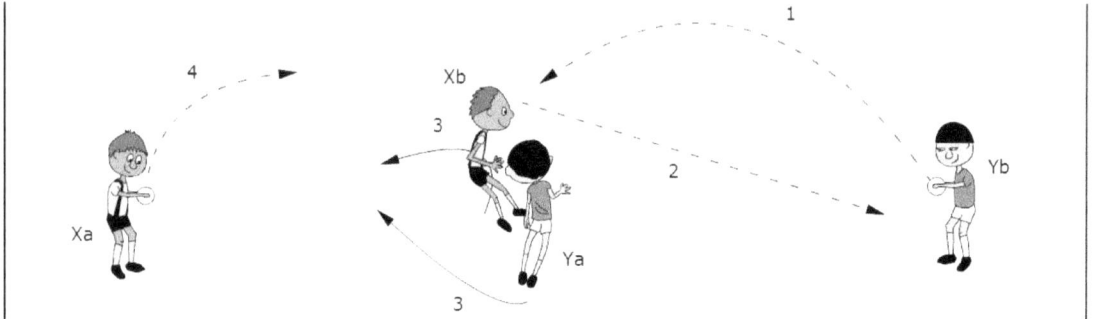

#1) Yb serves a neutral ball to Xb and Ya #2) Xb and Ya compete to return the ball to Yb
#3) Players merely turn around and compete for the next service from Xa.

Clearly this activity is aimed at age 11 and above. Keep score by teams. The first time this activity is used pair the players with similar courage and ability. On subsequent occasions players can make up their own teams. Play should not exceed 7 to 10 minutes. At later stages the same activity is used for continuing the ball forward using flicks.

Progress to the game of throw-head-catch for players 10 years and above. First as a possession game with two teams and finally across a goal line for scoring. Whenever the ball goes out of control, the team that picks it up first wins possession and the game proceeds. Eventually at age 12 or 13 players play a shortsided game with outside players serving balls to players for heading shots on goal. Start with hand service. Move to a game in which regular goals count 1 point but goals scored by headers count 5 points. This will provide incentive to head the ball.

Most teams really enjoy diving headers. Wet grass that is a little overgrown is perfect.

Research indicates that heading injuries are not so much from heading the ball, but from collisions among players when heading the ball. Quality officiating greatly protects players in all regards, but is especially important for heading collisions among players. Late arrivals and elbows up must be penalized.

The secret to success is not rushing the process. By building confidence all the way to game condition your players will not refuse heading in game situations, and in fact will take pride in performing the skill with excellence.

SPEED OF PLAY/ TRANSITION/QUICK COUNTER ATTACK

Throw and catch

This is a keep away game in which players use their hands to pass the ball to one another. This game permits tackling with the hands. Throw/Catch is often used to increase speed of play, although I once witnessed a Danish professional team use the game for a warm-up to a league match. I guess it was to relax them. They were having a blast doing it. In any case, instead of kicking the ball, the ball is thrown, allowing only 3 steps by the ball holder.

Opponents can tackle the ball carrier with their hands. Players love this game and it is also good for vision and support. When the ball hits the ground, whichever team retrieves the ball first wins possession. If a player intentionally holds the ball to get tackled this destroys the purpose of the game---simply remove the player from the game. Possibly a suggestion to get a drink of water and return when you want to implement the spirit of the game.

With older players the game is Throw/Head/Catch, in which a team can score by heading the ball over the endline of the grid to a teammate. However, the receiving player cannot be standing over the goal line, he can cross the endline only after the ball is headed to receive it and score a point. An obvious fringe benefit of this is learning how to deal with the offside rule.

There are many wrinkles to this game. One is no tackling and anyone who holds the ball for more than 3 seconds creates a turnover and the opponents are awarded the ball. This whole event must take place in less than five seconds or else the game meant to speed up play is being made useless.

Coaching points are getting open to support and looking long, playing short if necessary. Both close support and a distant open receiver should be available. This simulates forward long ball service or a long distance change in point of attack.

The lead up activity can be both teams using the entire grid hand passing and receiving with their own ball. By both teams being in the same area there is token defense, but still permitting a great deal of success. This will help perfect the physical skills of catching and throwing accurately. In turn this will help to make the competitive game much more effective in a much shorter period of time.

Occasionally a creative player, instead of catching the ball, will tap it to a teammate. If he is successful, compliment it, but generally it is not a good idea to encourage this to a whole team, as many are incapable of doing it successfully. Thus, the purpose of a controlled quick moving game is destroyed!

This game is also good for engendering the necessary body contact that soccer entails.

Quick Counter Attack

For ages 8 or above. Throw down a vest about 12 yards from the goal and whenever a player wins a ball in front of that vest any restriction that was in force for the shortsided game is abandoned and the player shoots directly or passes to a teammate instantly. In all cases a shot must be taken (attempted) with less than six touches of the ball. The number of allowed touches and distance of the vest is adjusted according to the coach's purpose (topic that day). The beauty of this technique is that it teaches quick counter attack in the most meaningful way imaginable and consumes zero amount of time. That's economical coaching at its best!

5 V 5 V 5 + 2 keepers

5v5v5+2 Keepers is a quick and fun transition game with fitness embedded into it. It can be played with player numbers of 2v2v2 to 6v6v6 with adjustment of the size of the field and the distance between the goals. For simplicity we have lime, orange and blue (L, B, O). The blue is attacking the orange team while the lime team waits at the other goal line. Here the field is divided in half, but sometimes divided into thirds with the requirement that the ball change point of attack in the middle third.

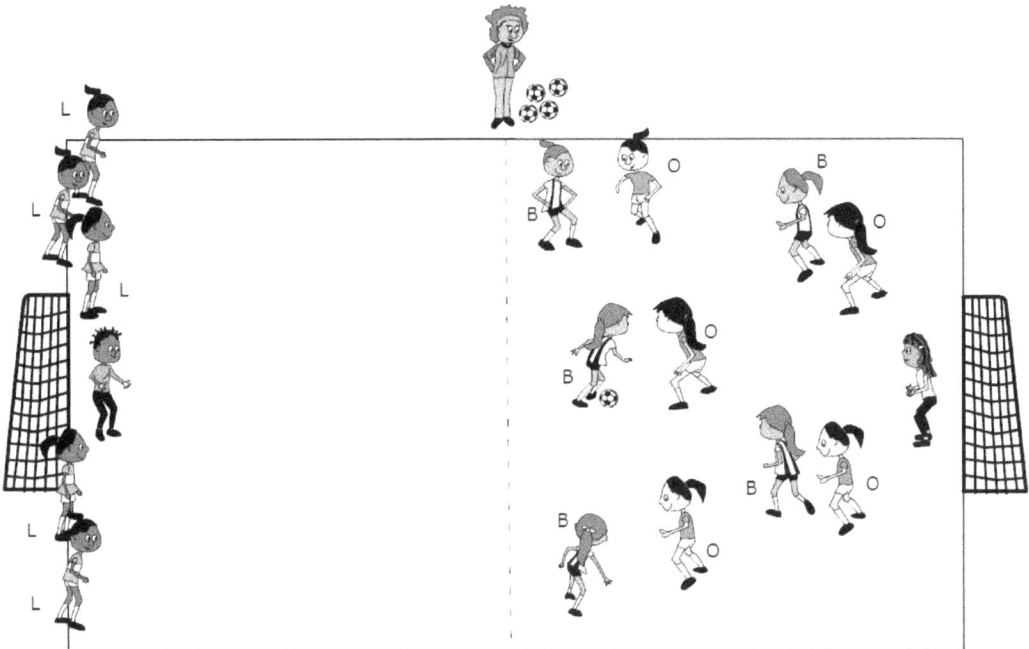

If blue scores they simply receive a ball from the coach and turn around and immediately attack the lime team to the left. If blue loses the ball, doesn't score or ball goes out of bounds off blue, orange attacks the lime team. Also if orange wins the ball they attack the lime team. Blue defends the goal they failed to score at. This is continuous exercise with the coach demanding rapid transition at the cost of assigning possession to ones opponents.

By having the waiting defending team relegated to the end line they must sprint forward to defend and yet slow down when approaching the opponent, assuming a low boxer stance. Keep team scores to maintain maximum competition and fun. Many different demands can be placed on the game related to the day's topic. Best to end with no demands to foster player creativity and fun.

For speed of play purposes, a number of touches restriction is imposed such as two touches. Plus or minus 10 total touches is another option. For other purposes the inducement can be a combination play or specifically a wall pass, the schemer (central midfielder) must touch the ball, the shot must be one touch, the shooter must beat someone before the shot, a cross must be executed, goals from headers count 3 points or whatever, the list is almost endless.

Occasionally a youngster may hold the ball on throw-ins, disrupting the flow of the game. A simple remedy is to award the other team the ball and the problem is resolved quickly without any time wasted or any unnecessary admonishment. If questioned you called a delay of game foul. At the same time this technique fosters the quick throw-in, and of course more fun for the entire group. The ball holding behavior eventually causes the bad habit of teammates not making runs to be open to receive. Some confuse having the option of a quick throw-in with doing it mindlessly all the time. Maximum throw-in success results from a wide variety---that is, DOING WHAT THE SITUATION CALLS FOR. Players should be ready for a quick throw-in, but it should only be used when appropriate, that is when a player is open, your team is behind, you see a great run by a teammate, etc.

Throw-in Tactic: In the final third the two scorers go into the best scoring location possible and the throw-in receiver is instructed to immediately cross the ball to the goalmouth area. This is no time for a lot of passing, wasting time or any behavior that can cause the team to lose the ball before they obtain service. This is Nike time, "Just Do It!". Get it done as quickly and as simply as possible. Why chance losing the ball? If a team can get service, get it done!

3 v 1 Breakout

An extremely simple breakout activity is to have 3v1 in one or more grids depending upon the number of players available. Place the grids about 20 yards from the goal. Grids should be generous---12 x 12 to ensure success.

Players are required to make three passes and then a player breaks out on the dribble accompanied by one teammate and the defender. The first priority is to score off the initial dribble! Alternate the defender on every trial. In the grid the offense will have it best chances for success by maintaining the triangle shape. If the defender wins the ball he shoots with only one offensive player defending. In breakout the entire focus is to create a shot as fast as possible, then take that shot!

Make sure players retrieve balls quickly and are ready to go as soon as possible. While waiting for the competitive turn to attack, the other grid players do not stand and wait, but instead all four players (3 offensive and the single defender) are all passing the ball to one another. Once the other group has shot, the defender calls, "Ready!", then defends, and the three passes requirement is in effect and the attack on goal begins.

For younger groups have no defender and require continuous passing until the coach says, "Group 1 shoot", then a maximum two passes is in effect. There are many options such as: 1) only two touches out of the grid before a shot, 2) two players leave the grid and one must prepare a shot for the other with all shots being one touch, 3) you must beat the keeper before a shot, 4) a player leaves and goes to the endline and crosses for a teammate to finish (left side goes left, right side goes right), 5) shot must be off a through pass, 6) a wall pass demand. Much depends upon the topic of the day. Clearly some options are for the upper ranges of the age levels covered throughout the text. Also some are not exactly breakout quick transition tactics.

The simplest form of quick counter attack is to play soccer with the restriction that X number of passes or touches must not be exceeded before a shot. This tactical instruction method is inappropriate for ages 5-9 and only accomplished teams above those ages would find this technique appropriate. The reason is that this is only sensible after players can possess the ball well, play combinations, build out of the back and do what the game score demands. If a team cannot hold the ball for extended periods of time when they are up in the score, quick counter attack instruction will probably retard all those more basic tactics.

It is never too early to begin good transition tactics habits. Good habits begin in training, and in this case moving from one activity to another must be efficient. Substituting positions of sideline players being done on the fly will also cause better transitions and increase training time.

In general do not allow constant stoppages and delays needlessly. It just establishes bad habits. "Talk less, do more" is the motto of youth coaching in order to establish muscle memory through repetition. Obviously, water breaks and making a coaching point are done with purpose of clarity and brevity. Coaching points made for more than a minute disrupt playing so much that nearly all possible benefits are lost. One college coach in a recent article said he restricts his coaching points to 7 seconds. That may be a bit extreme, but it gives the youth coach some idea how career coaches think and act.

POSSESSION

For the very youngest players one of the first levels of possession is the team playing keep away from the coach. If there are more than 8 players at the session consider two groups. With a single group use two balls for additional ball touches. Of course the coach does not make a full effort. When the team gets a bit competent, probably not before age 7, a player can be substituted for the coach to play against the whole team.

Clarified earlier, the 3v0 that evolves into 3v1 is a staple for possession.

Specific number(s) of touches aid the development of different skills. For example:
- Two touch fosters control before the pass or shot
- Three touch sets up experience for: control the ball, beat someone with a move, and the third touch is a shot, pass, service or cross
- Four or more touches generally is an attempt to develop composure and dribbling skills in game situations such as break-aways

One touch is generally done for speed of play, developing support, although it is not emphasized here because it will cause mindless play for young players. One touch exercises are for older accomplished teams.

Quality Decisions

This is a lead up activity for mindful possession: Four players are arranged as shown.

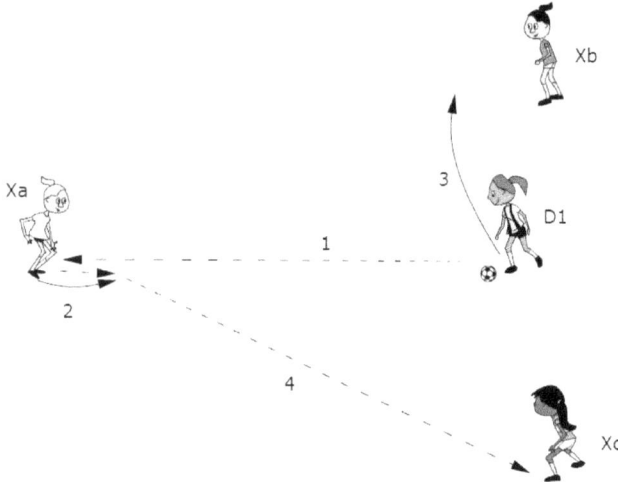

D has the ball to start: #1 D passes to Xa: #2 Xa uses one touch to prepare the ball for a pass to either Xb or Xc; Xa passes on the second touch # 3 during the first touch the defender D1 moves to completely mark either Xb or Xc (in this case she is completely defending against Xb): #4 therefore Xa passes to the 'open man' Xc, having made a correct decision.

Each player gets to all locations for about 10 trials. Simple clockwise rotation is employed. In this way the basic idea of passing to the open player is initiated. If necessary a parent or the coach can be the defender since that role is only there to facilitate the decision making of the Xa location. This will also allow two groups to be working if the number of players allows for it. Be sure the defender does not go to Xb or Xc in a predictable manner. The defender must move in a random fashion so that Xa must look and make the correct decision.

Progression Option: Xa passes one touch, in which case D marks either Xb or Xc immediately after passing the ball.

2 + 4 Neutrals vs 2 Defenders

In this exercise the neutrals offer offensive help to make possession successful even for beginners. Essentially this is a 6v2 exercise. Almost any numbers will work, just adjust the number of outside neutrals for the number of players available. Outside neutrals have two touches.

1V1 With Circle Support for Possession

Two players playing 1v1 attempt to maintain possession by dribbling and using the outside players for passing support. Outside players are restricted to two touches, thus the inside player who passed the ball must move to get open to receive the return pass.

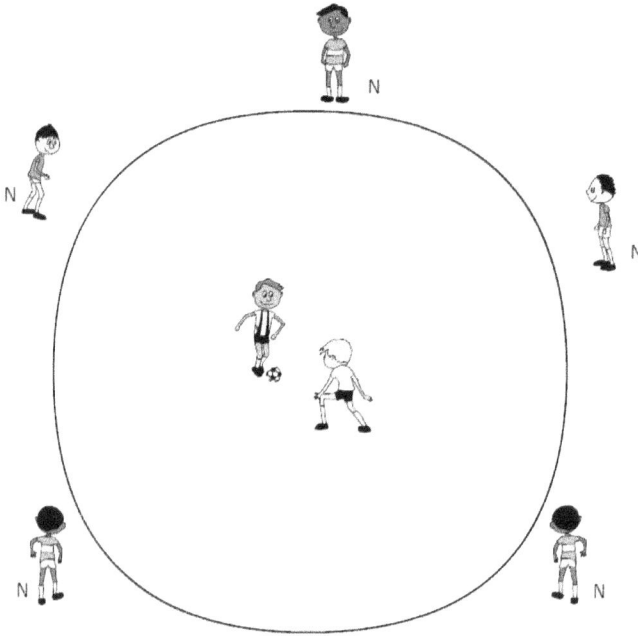

N

N

N

N

N

N

Allowing this support facilitates possession for very young players. Possession is so important that we must begin the rudiments of it at an early age. This could also be 2v1, 2v2 or even a 3v1 exercise.

At age 10-12 more traditional two team possession activities can occur. To facilitate success include a neutral for the team in possession. For complete treatment of possession see "Soccer Coaching Principles of Technical and Tactical Development" seen in the bibliography. It has an entire comprehensive chapter on more than a dozen prototype possession activities.

3V1+2 with movement

There are two 12 x 12 yard grids side by side. This is an excellent possession game because it involves movement. Possession games that lack movement can be negative due to the unnatural lack of game movement.

X's play possession while Ya defends. When Y wins the ball he passes to his teammates on the right and they play possession against one X defender. Note the waiting players are somewhat deep in their grid to allow an easy first pass and to give time for Ya to come to their aid. Also the X player will have more distance to travel giving Y's more time to gain control of the ball and arrange their shape. Adjust the grid size to your players' needs. Whenever the possession team makes 3 passes they score a point, 6 passes is 2 points, etc.

Get players to keep score out loud so that you know they are really competing! For ages 12 and above this activity is usually 3v2 + 1 or 4v2 + 2.

For 5v2 and similar keep away possession, Fidgi Haig, a local college coach, sometimes has no grid and the entire group must adjust to whatever happens to the ball. When an errant pass sends the ball 10-20 yards away the group moves. That's game related! Naturally a grid size must be maintained. Not recommended here as it is too difficult for beginners. Age 13 through adult level.

CHECKING

Checking is an important skill in order to get free for support and possession. A simple introductory format is shown. Checking can be 'checking to' or 'checking away' which sometimes involves going over the top, getting behind the defense. Both are best accomplished by a sharp jab step that changes direction and angle.

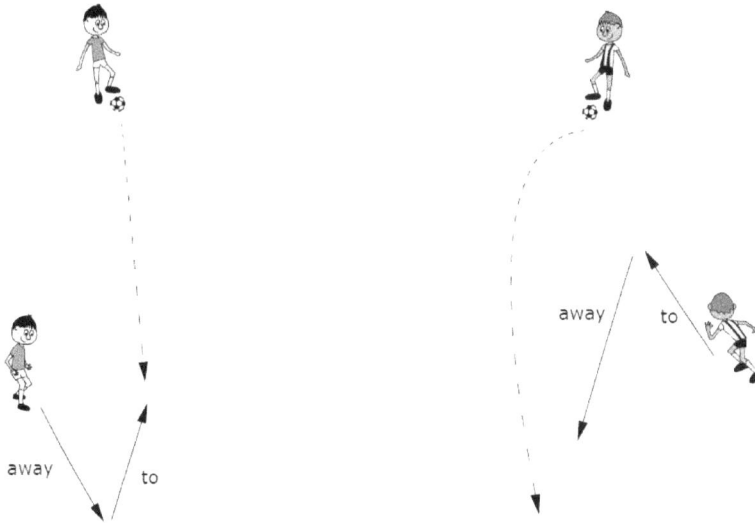

To start there is no defender. Later on success is greatly enhanced by the player initiating slight contact with the defender and moving a significant distance. Eye contact and pointing improves the quality of the pass connection. Note checking in both directions is done at an angle.

Exercise: The server raises her hand and when she drops her hand the player begins checking. Checking is done with a jab step in order to lose the defender. If the change in direction is not sharp an attacker will not lose the defender. The server does not stand with a still ball, instead he does Basic (touching the ball back and forth between the two feet), short dribbles back and forth, toe taps, etc. prior to service.
Rotate the roles.

Side-on checking is another form of getting free from a defender. Side-on checks merely have the attacker use a slight shoulder charge bump and then move away in the opposite direction to receive the ball.

Summary: Knowledgeable coaches of ages 11 through adults seldom have a training session without one of the dozens of possibilities of possession exercises. Two teams, three or four teams, grids, circles, target players, schemer neutrals, twin striker pairing, two and three touch situations, 3v1, 4v2, 5v2, combination play emphasis, the list of the variety of possession exercises is almost limitless.

Move to a restricted game and finally free play. Free play is meant to give adequate freedom to players to foster their individuality and creativity. If you only see what your progression was focused on once in the free play be pleased with your success.

TEAM SHAPE

One way to teach young players team shape versus the infantile notion of positions is to set up about 4 or 5 more cones than the team formation used in the team's games. The example is done for youngsters playing 8 aside with 7 field players and a keeper. Semi-ignoring the keeper's position in the cone arrangement, let's assume the team is playing K-3-3-1. Formations are always indicated starting from the back to forward positions. No matter what the shape, the cones are laid out in a fashion similar to that shape, but with extra cones. In this case twelve cones for eight aside player matches.

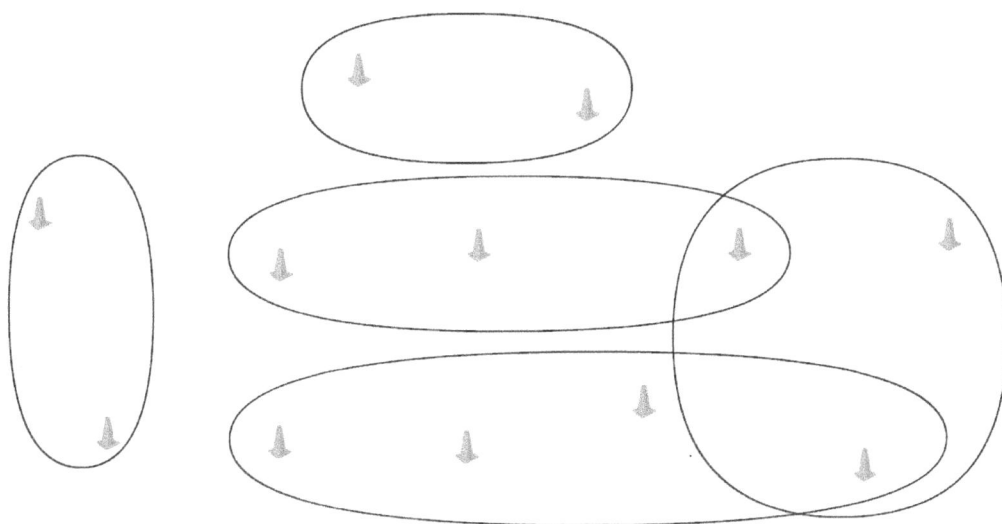

If at any time one of these circled areas is unoccupied simply stop the activity and ask the team if they think this would be good positioning (shape) for the team.

Use of this activity: Players dribble to a new cone, leave the ball there for their teammate to dribble to another vacant cone, and stay at that cone or go to any vacant cone that will help the team keep an overall good shape. If youngsters have already been taught a proper takeover, they can do a takeover. This process goes on continuously. As soon as players get the idea, add another ball to increase the touches and visual skills.

The entire session continues in this structure while adding a couple of the following items. Over several 15 to 18 minute sessions a coach could do the full progression listed below.
• Move to a pass and go to a new cone
• Passing with two balls
• Skip passes, this is a very important and useful option of the activities listed (Emphasize movements that your team has already somewhat developed)

- Move to wall passes, probably one ball
- Use overlaps; unlikely successful until age ten or beyond

After the suggested options players can perform any movement of their own choosing. Start with one ball and move to two balls.

The entire progression has little or no coaching except when the team shape is poor, that is: 1) no strikers, 2) one side completely vacant, 3) less than 2 defenders in the back, 4) no one in either of the central areas.

Stop and ask the team shape question:
"Do you think playing in this shape is good for our success?"

Similar question stoppages: "Do we want to play without strikers?" or whatever the case may be. The players will on their own start to creep or move to a better shape. Having used this activity dozens of times I am certain that the players will improve their shape on their own! Because players have so much ownership of the decision making in this activity, the carry over to games is quite good. Breaking up the bee swarm in a positive manner is no easy task. Doing it in a positive way such as this is a great accomplishment.

Don't allow the creeping until everyone sees the poor team shape. Once everyone has seen it, allow the creeper (the advanced thinker), to improve the team shape.

Another method to teach team shape and break up the bee swarm is 'Touch Cones', seen on the next page. Try to view the bee swarm for ages 4-7 as a plus because it means the child wants the ball and is willing to go to it. At approximately age 9 the first law of offense, which is to spread out when your team is in possession must begin to take hold. For that reason the previous and following exercises are clarified here.

Touch Cones

About 6 cones spread throughout the field, possibly two on the field and four on the perimeter as shown in the diagram. Almost any arrangement of cones will help players to pass and move. Players are required after every pass to move to and touch a cone.

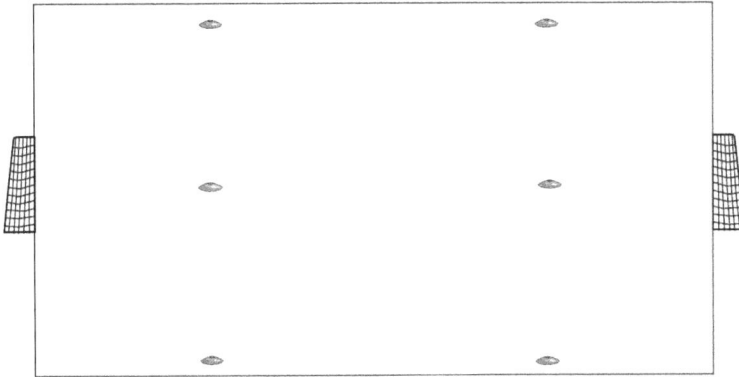

After each pass the player is required to pass and move. The move must be touch one of the cones placed on the field. In time hopefully players will go to the cone that best supports the ball, but of course in time the coach can instruct this if it does not happen naturally.

These activities do away with much of the annoying screaming about positioning during the game. Furthermore, parents must be notified that they are not to yell out such instructions no matter what the cost. Yelling at players is not cheering, it is coaching, and is not the parents' role. With an excess of players there could be a requirement to pass to outside neutrals or run to the outside neutral and then the neutral comes onto the field to take the place of the player that left. These are constructive ways to break up the bee swarm instead of destroying players' thinking. At the same time it raises their level of decision making. That is a win, win situation.

Also see in the section of Shortsided Games; 3v3 Playing Wide and Channel Play.

Very little is ever accomplished in a single session, so this requires several sessions with review of previous demands and new wrinkles provided by the coach. Much higher versions of this can occur for the 11-a-side game for ages 12 and beyond with movement up and down the field. Even professional coaches spend some time in training their teams for a proper shape for various situations. In a general way, all systems demand the same thing. Open up on offense, stay compact on defense!

PRESSURE TRAINING

Pressure training is nothing more than a requirement of performing a skill when tired. While it nearly always taxes the fitness of the player it often also forces quick decisions and even develops mental strength. Generally it is only considered for high levels, but many youngsters also enjoy the challenge that basic pressure training presents.

Pressure Passing

One player receives passes from 4 servers. Each of the servers has a ball and a small grid about 2 yards square is in the center as shown. S = servers

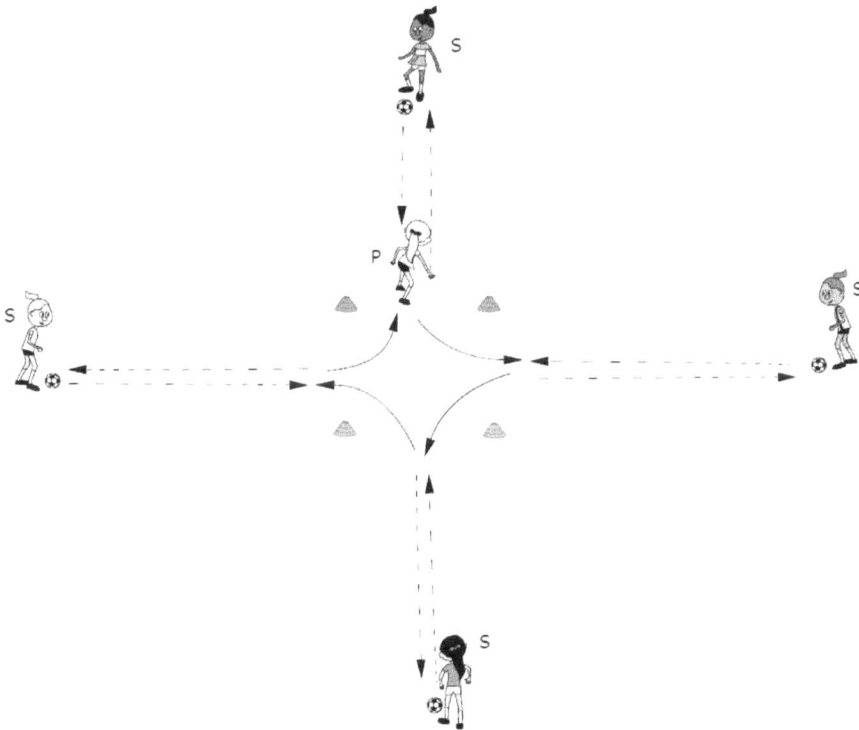

P is the player being pressure trained for executing the inside of the push pass under pressure. Servers serve a slow ground push pass that P must return to the server with a single touch then run through the cone grid to do the same with the next server. This action is done continuously.

Generally it is difficult to get the servers to serve a properly paced ball to the player being pressure trained. Success will come, but it takes a bit of an effort by the coach to get young players to learn how to serve a properly paced ball for a teammate to run onto. Timing when the pass is to be made is also a challenge. The server should serve the ball when the player enters the grid.

Usually after a minute the pressure player is exhausted. While this is a not a conditioning exercise, players are being conditioned. Keep in mind that its primary purpose is to develop quality technical skill while in a tired condition. Of course the servers are also perfecting the push pass at the same time. The player just keeps on going to the next server and returning the push pass one touch. Be certain the player continues to move to the ball without stopping. As always, eye contact between the passer and receiver is required. Do not accept back pedaling; make sure the player is turning and running. This works best when the servers are about 15 yards distant from the grid. The slow pass must be DEMANDED so that the pressure player is truly receiving pressure training by having to move some distance to the ball.

Shooting pressure training is also common. One method is to place 10 balls at the 18 yard line. The distance is adjusted to the level of the player. Six year olds are often asked to take the shots from 10 yards away.

Sometimes the keeper is trained by having many successive shots. That is usually done with the coach shooting so that the keeper with effort can make the save.

A dribbling relay can also be used as pressure training by having long relays with many repetitions.

Like many training formats pressure training can be over done. A case in point is allowing sloppy technical execution while using pressure training for fitness.

Actually almost all smallsided games involve pressure training as it is very demanding to play 1v1 or even 2, 3, or 4 aside on an appropriate size field.

You can take many of the activities in this text and use them for fitness by merely demanding a good effort while players are tired.

Cross-training at the younger age levels can increase interest in your program. While ladders, hoops, obstacle courses, small gates, body weight activities, stretching, medicine ball exercises are not discouraged, possibly there are other equal or more interesting cross training methods. Certainly isolated fitness without the ball is not encouraged for ages 4-11. Even many high level coaches only do fitness with the ball. However Over-the-Net tennis tournaments, bicycle riding sessions, beach soccer volleyball, a whole session of a 3v3 tournament, shootout contests, relay contests with the ball, might be more motivating to our young players.

The realm of fitness is vastly misunderstood due to the history of running being the main component for developing fitness. Unfortunately it makes no sense for youngsters who are not yet competent with the ball to be running to nowhere. Instead, they should be developing fitness while also developing soccer skills. Children, who generally run until out of gas, rest, and then run again until exhausted, have the perfect built in mechanism of interval training that is the highest level format of fitness training. Why ruin it by mindless group running? Good youth coaches run vigorous practices with technical/ tactical ball activities, shortsided games which are enormously rigorous, with scrimmages demanding quality support with off the ball positioning, and combination play; all of which have very high demands on fitness. All the experts agree that with youth all fitness training is done with the ball.

It seems that only when we pay players millions of dollars do they learn how to cheat in regard to fitness and so coaches at that level must require runs of predetermined distances, time framed activities and other artificial means of developing fitness!

GOALKEEPING

This is not an exhaustive review of the large array of goalkeeping skills. For an excellent synopsis with quality activities see **Soccer Coaching: Principles of Technical and Tactical Development**. It contains a goalkeeping chapter that includes all the important skills of goalkeeping with over 45 photos to clearly demonstrate the skill.

Here the only concern is that all players get a turn to be goalkeeper because it is unbelievably revealing to go in goal and attempt to make saves. Not only does being the goalkeeper reveal the many skills of the position, it also makes it clear how much courage it requires. The exploration of the position by everyone allows those who care to assume this role to get a feeling for it. Again the educational aspect of youth soccer takes precedence over winning the game. By the same token, all players get to play in the field and acquire field players skills, which is so necessary for the modern goalkeeper.

Also, getting to play all positions is an excellent learning opportunity. By age 14 or 15 players can settle into a given position, but it is surprising how often in high school, college and even in professional ranks players are converted to a new position. Becoming an all around soccer player is important. A player may be a good striker, but end up on a team with two better strikers. If the team is playing a two man front and he cannot play elsewhere he may be sitting on the bench. This is sad and unnecessary if the player is one of the top ten players on the team. Often players who are insisting they belong in a specific position are only repeating what a parent, previous coach or some other outside source has said to them, and in many cases this is faulty information.

That being said, it is not a matter of throwing players into unfamiliar positions haphazardly, thinking that is good instruction. It is not. Instead, over the course of their youth playing career, give or take 5 years (possibly 10 seasons) between ages 4 and 13, players should be given some insights into the various positions on the field. Generally a season will be more than adequate for the youngster to learn quite a bit about a given position. By seeing the whole field from the defensive position players often improve their reading of the game. The tight space and body contact in the midfield is another valuable experience. Playing with his back to the goal, a striker learns serious checking and other skills not widely used in other positions. There are dozens of other benefits to learning the various positions in soccer. This is true because the mobility in soccer, team shape instead of positions, places everyone in the various roles during an actual game. Strikers must defend, wingbacks must serve balls and anyone may have a chance for a shot!

In any case the most basic skills of goalkeeping are: Catching, dealing with crosses, breakaways, punting, goal kicks, various hand distributions, and to a lesser extent special situations. Moving forward, leading with the hands is important for safety and good goalkeeping. Clear positive communication of "Keeper" or "Away" is an excellent communication habit to acquire early in one's goalkeeping experience.

Another area of concern is intentional body contact with field players. This has no place in the game. It is especially dangerous when the head is kept down, as this places the spine in a straight condition. This type of collision by a keeper can lead to serious injury. Spinal breaks are never inconsequential. It can even be fatal or cause paralysis.

In any case, the goalkeeping position is just as important as any other position and has special skills that players should be exposed to during the exploratory golden years of learning.

There are various "Get Set" positions, but for youth the one that best protects the face is the one shown here. A keeper always wants to be in the "Get Set" position prior to the shot, even if they are not in the best possible location at that point in time.

Here the keeper is showing us a good hand position for catching. Sometimes referred to as the "W" or "O" Catch. The main point is to be certain to have the youngster have the hands well behind the ball so it does not go through and end up in the goal.

Here the keeper is practicing hand distribution to a target, in this case a small goal. Main throws are; a rolling ground ball and the overhand long air ball, which should not be spinning, should be somewhat of a line drive to arrive at its destination quickly. The biggest coaching problem is getting youngsters to step to the target and follow through properly.

When going after an air ball the knee is lifted on the side where a charge is coming from by a field player. The knee protects the keeper and the ability to hold the ball. The knee lift also helps propel the keeper higher in the air.

A great way to get a lot of practice is by finding a wall and catching, throwing, punting, goal kicks, heading, reaction saves and just getting great confidence in handling the ball. The wall is great because it causes many repetitions in a short period of time. Furthermore youngsters learn how to "coach" themselves.

Here we see the keeper intentionally avoiding a direct collison. Head is up keeping the spinal chord in a safe curved position as opposed to putting the head down, thus endangering the spine. Note how well the keepers has tucked the ball safely in upper abdominal area so that the ensuing fall forward has the ball well secured.

Here the keeper is working on forward movement, but incorporating sideways shuffle as there are many occasions that requires the keeper to change direction. At times there is a great necessity for moving off the line in order to make a save. It always adds enthusiasm and hard work when a save is demanded after shuffling forward because the keeper sees how the shuffling is game related.

Here the keeper is making a forward collapse dive and simultaneously is bringing the ball to the "bread basket" (abdominal area) for safety. The impact with the ground will be minimal so as not to have the ball pop out; this is so because the keeper is low, feet on the ground, then knees gently contacting the surface and finally the thighs and arms. The tendency of inexperienced keepers is to not get low, then the impact is severe increasing the danger of the ball being dislodged.

Providing many catches of the ball in a variety of ways is at the top of the list of what to do with the beginning goalkeeper. Throwing is also important, especially due to the reduced size field for young players. "Get Set" is a good skill to develop early on. The most important skill for good goalkeeping is the habit of moving forward and leading the body with the hands.

This chapter has been by no means an exhaustive discussion on all of the possible skills and exercises for the goalkeeper, but merely an introduction to the most fundamental aspects of the role, with a great deal of emphasis on safety.

For those of you who would like to delve further into the topic of goalkeeping, there are many excellent resources available for all levels of play. Online, Reedswain.com has an expansive collection of goalkeeping related dvds and books from top coaches around the world.

SELF TRAINING

When discussing this area with players it is best to refer to it as something other than "homework", which for many children carries a negative connotation. Instead, use positive terms such as "On your own play", "fun development", "things to do on your own", "personal soccer growth", etc. The main job of the youth coach is to make sure the players have enough fun to continue to play soccer, derive enough enjoyment from the game to touch the ball on their own and take personal ownership of their game. Constant reminders of little at-home assignments will greatly help players to develop themselves. Without exception the players who become accomplished do some soccer ball activities on their own. Suggestions from the coach just help players get an idea of what they can do to further their development. Possible activities are:

- Juggling record keeping by the coach or an assistant will motivate players to practice their juggling on their own. Recording this one at a time so no training time is wasted works well. This is another example of the necessity for coaching assistants! Never compare one player to another, only offer encouragement for the individual's growth even if it is from 2 to 3 juggles.
- Kicking against a kicking wall, a pitch-back, handball court, flat faced goal or cement block or brick wall with no windows
- Shooting on goal using a prepared touch, turning, dribbling around obstacles
- 1v1 games with anyone. Also, 2v1, 1v2, 2v2 etc. Playing is always outstanding practice. Encouraging sub-groups of the team that live near each other to get together sometimes works well.
- If there are pickup games of any kind, encourage attendance. In our area we have 3-a-side pickup tournaments on Friday nights. If no such programs exist in your area, you could encourage the initiation of such a program in your club.
- My daughter set up a field in the basement and played games in the cold snowy winter months. Fortunately she used a nerf soccer ball! Indoor soccer of course is a great help to player development.
- Suggest that players bring a ball to school so that they can have recess or lunch time games
- Watching games, especially if you are lucky enough to have a local college or professional team nearby; male or female is irrelevant. Sometimes there is a very high level state team playing locally. Any of these can be worthwhile experiences.
- Sometimes the best way to encourage practice away from the team sessions is to ask players what they do and/or what they think will be a good idea for improvement by working on their own

Most importantly, do not make self-training drudgery. Encourage and reward those who do things on their own, but avoid rigid demands in this area. Sometimes just recording players' activities at practice in front of them will encourage "on their own soccer". While the ball touches aspect is a great help, taking ownership of one's game is of equal importance.

In interviews, professional players frequently mention that they spent thousands of hours with the ball on their own. Personal practice has elements in it that can never be matched by a coach. What we try to do is to come as close as we can to having a youngster take ownership of the game (develop themselves).

These guys are serious. They are going to play soccer no matter how difficult the situation is to find a place to play. I guess the two rags are the goal.

This sort of thing is starting to happen in some places. Our soldiers in Iraq and Afghanistan have been playing pick up games in-between their more troublesome duties. Unfortunately wars have always promulgated sports. Civil War baseball, WWI football, WWII basketball; hopefully there will be more positive ways for soccer to grow in the USA.

TECHNIQUE LISTING

This is nothing more than a reminder of the many technical skills that the coach may choose to train. Some are technical/tactical because some are difficult to separate the two aspects from one another. By no means does this listing cover all the possible technical skills a high level player possesses. Hopefully it covers the vast majority of important techniques.

Technique is clearly the first dimension for becoming an accomplished player. It usually has a great effect on decision making in both individual and small group tactics. It also plays a huge role in mental confidence, often referred to as psychology. However, quality player development demands the integration of techniques in tactical games! I certainly reject the idea that there are no tactics without technique because some players help themselves a great deal by making good decisions such as being in the right place to support, cover or to score. Nonetheless, to reach the higher levels of the game quality technique is a must. Certainly mental toughness and fitness further add major dimensions to a player's technical and tactical development. Granted, players with strengths in all four areas are rare, and they generally enjoy great success in the game of soccer.

Individual tactics, small group tactics (mostly two man combinations) and team tactics are all very different from one another. When some experts downgrade the importance of tactical instruction at early ages they are referring to team tactics. Team tactics includes team formation, positioning and functional training, which is the special training required for a specific position. That's all well and good. However, individual tactics decisions must be attended to at all ages for all players. A youngster of 6 or 7 years of age should learn early on that if no pass is available she should attempt to dribble in order to find a receiver or shot! The terrible habit of kicking a ball to nowhere with no intent or purpose is a difficult one to break at a later stage of development.

Also, young players often simply do not have the techniques necessary for many team tactics. Simple examples are the inability to strike the ball long distances for crosses to the far post, long range shooting, defenders hitting target players and a myriad of other techniques that are not yet developed. Chips and flicks are out of the question for very young players. The maximum developmental maturational period for technique is from ages 5-12, especially since this is by far the best period for solo play, which is a major ingredient of abundant ball contact and therefore of technique. Virtually all experts agree on that. However, when two small children of 6 years of age play 1 vs 1, a number of decisions abound. Should I dribble, shield, feint, go at speed to beat the defender, nutmeg? Which particular move should I make or whatever are all individual decisions (tactics) that are important. In any case, most instructors, clinicians and knowledgeable coaches feel that the great emphasis should be on technique in the early stages of development and involve tactics to a greater extent as the player gains technical competence. The concept of introducing some small group tactics of wall passes, takeovers, overlaps and third man-on is more controversial, but this text has clearly indicated that combination play must be integrated into the child's program early on. Why? Because all of these movements demand movement on and off the ball, thereby initiating mobility which so many youngsters lack as a result of doing isolated technique training. Still, playing employs all the elements of the game and therefore must be a large part of training time. Playing always involves techniques and tactics in an integrated fashion.

When competitive games are included with the restricted playing, about 50% or more of the practice time should be consumed in playing. The stark reality is that separating technique and tactics is nearly impossible since the only way to develop a player for soccer is to play the game.

The period of solo play is far more prevalent during the early ages and must be exploited. Ages four through twelve provide the best opportunity for the countless number of touches that are required to become an excellent player. Unfortunately, too much coaching in these early years can deter a youngster from the game, but if poor habits are established during this period of time they are hard to change. Therefore, a very delicate balance of introducing proper technique and allowing players to play and have fun is necessary.

Generally, shortsided games will greatly aid decision making, though all phases of the game must be taught. Certainly, economical training of introducing a specific technique such as the inside of the foot push pass and then using the technique in a wall pass environment can aid the relationship of technique and tactics. This placed in a shortsided game with strong encouragement, or even a restriction of playing a wall pass before going to goal can add integrated technical/tactical fitness and mental toughness.

There are numerous techniques, as seen from the list that follows. However, with patience, doing one at a time there is more than enough opportunity to teach many of the techniques and revisit each topic several times before the player is approximately fourteen years of age. Of course, even at the professional level these techniques are performed in warm-up and even rehearsed in relation to a given team tactic.

Repetition is obviously the foundation of technique, and abundant hours of shortsided games of 3v1, 2v1, 1v1, 1v2, 3v2, 2v2, 3v3, 4v2, etc. in many different environments will help to make it a SKILL. It is important to recall that a technique capably performed in a game situation is a skill.

Note many skills are taught at more than one level. The levels are a very crude guideline. Almost all are revisited at all levels.

BEGINNERS:
- Going to the ball: must be a constant in all activities and games; separate from checking
- Choosing the correct surface to collect
- Collection through the ball; movement with ball
- Crossing; for beginners this is usually short distance ground balls
- Combo play techniques: wall passes, takeovers, overlaps; especially technical features
- Collection away from pressure; using various surfaces
- Repetition of all the Coerver Moves (Pull-a-V, Sole Roll, Scissor, Step Over, etc.)
- Dribbling: for safety, away from pressure
- Dribbling to beat someone
- Decision Grid: Decision maker passing exercise clarified in text
  Inside of foot push pass, "HAT"
- Receiving: foot, thigh, chest, head, abdominal (hand service competence precedes foot service for receiving); move to foot service once hand service competence is well established
- Shooting: off the dribble, two touch, on the turn; one touch emphasis on low driven balls for all ages
- Turns: Cruyff, scissor, sole roll, chop, outside of foot hook move, 360 degrees, other moves
- Weak foot development, especially eventually in game situation
- Juggling: ball control; start with permitting a bounce; advanced to no bounce, higher distances, changes of direction; also high to low, low to high touches, heading touches, outside and inside of the foot usage, recognize little innovations displayed by individual players

INTERMEDIATE:
- Bent runs for proper angle of reception
- Blindside runs
- Chipping
- Checking to the ball, strong jab step
- Bump check
- Banana kick (also reverse banana kick)

- Creating Space, player leaving a space for another player to occupy
- Defending with and without cover; simple introduction below age 11
- Channel development; passing to, receiving (running onto a pass), creating
- Driving; speed dribble, especially to shoot or cross
- Feinting: for shot, to receive, pass or head
- Heading; down for passing or shooting, up for clearing
- Heel Pass: parallel, cross legged
- Half volleys; still keeping the ball down
- Full Volleys: side-on, straight forward
- Dummying the pass or shot
- Constantly peeking over the shoulder
- One Touch: whole body execution, incorporating balance
- Layoff: frequently inside of foot, one touch, ground, to dominant foot
- Lofted ball serving
- Power Instep Drive: shots, service (driven, lofted)
- Recovery runs: see man and ball, hips facing proper direction
- Shielding; also combat games to facilitate comfort with body contact
- Shooting: exciting games, Carolina, Bull Pen, Kings, many used often
- Shooting one touch; coming from, square, forward, all types of diagonal passes
- Side-on receiving; open hips to teammates
- Spreading yourself: arms out, make yourself big, low, feet shoulder width, balanced
- Spin Out; without ball or after pass
- Spin turn with ball
- Tackling, recover tackle, getting up from ground
- Third man-on movement
- Throw-in technique
- Toe Pokes, too early an introduction could interfere with push pass and power instep drive
- Vision training: color possession games, and basic vision concepts (well covered throughout the text)
- Pass to ones self and go around
- Takeover
- Wall Pass
- Overlap

ADVANCED:
- Flicking: for passing, shooting, feet/head
- Bicycle kick (scoring, passing, clearing)
- Catching ball on foot

- Chop collection; puts back spin on ball for close control
- Diving headers
- Juggling: 3v1 keep away in 10 yard grid
- Nut Meg; off opponent for corner kick or throw-in
- Top spin shots that cause the ball to dip down
- Reverse banana kick over long distance; outside of the foot, bent L to R with right foot
- Bent runs to open hips and see maximum number of teammates and opponents
- On sides running; square, east/west, cut to goal, not until server serves the ball
- Air dribbling, especially with movement

Try desperately to end with unrestricted play for a significant amount of time. In fact, if you fail, the next session should begin with a very brief review of the restricted shortsided game, and immediately move to the free playing game. The review and lapse in time may actually be a plus. Many of us do not do enough review and yet most of us are more than aware of the necessity for repetition. Research which substantiates the spiral curriculum is very definite about returning to an item with a lapse in time. Certainly there are times where block learning is vital in order to gain emphasis, but the spiral (elapse time, review, return to topic at future date----cyclical instruction) is clearly the preferred method of teaching for retention according to numerous studies!

In view of the technique listing above, you'll never run out of topics for your future training sessions, especially when you consider the additional needs for tactical topics, fitness, and general coordination/agility needs.

An extremely important point that is often not adequately emphasized is that, to be successful, teams must attack and defend as a unit. Leaving anyone disconnected from the team's effort in either regard is poor playing and if condoned by the coach is poor coaching. Big spaces give opponents too much time to develop quality strategies of attack and also allow attackers to come at a defense with speed. When a player approaches at speed and the defender is standing still, or even worse moving toward the offensive player, the big advantage goes to the attacking player. A single deep player also leaves a situation where cover, an essential element of defense, is nearly impossible. The concept of team play is unity in attack, defense and transition.

At higher levels this connecting is referred to as linking, a key component of good teams. Starting the correct habit with youth players saves an enormous amount time later in player development.

DEVELOPMENTAL VS DIAGNOSTIC INSTRUCTION

Developmental learning is simply the notion that we teach all the players the same basic skills. Diagnostic instruction is for high levels where the game is an enormous part of the instruction garnered from game performances. With ages 4-10 it is much more like kindergarten where we teach all the children the alphabet and later on separate them for their appropriate level of reading. This does not mean we ignore game performance, but in general there is little that the players can do so they all need dribbling, passing/receiving, tackling, shooting and eventually heading. We have little concern for focusing on a given position, referred to as functional training which comes into much more prominence at ages beyond twelve.

In regard to game plans with youth, the plan is always developmental, that is the game plan is whatever we trained for that week. The game plan is not necessarily related to the opponent's strength or weaknesses, but instead if we worked on wall passes this week, the goal might be to perform two wall passes in each half of the game. This can be stated to players at the last practice before the game, just before the game, at half time and the success or failure should be mentioned at the post game review at the next practice. In this way the coach's eye is always clearly on development. If development truly occurs there will be many successful results of games in the future.

If what is trained for is not discussed in relation to the game, players quickly surmise training is not important. You didn't intend that, but youngsters are quick to pick up those signals.

Sports psychology is mostly covered by merely being positive. If one wanted to delve a bit further into this topic the main concerns would be to focus on performance goals instead of outcome goals and teach focus techniques and visualization as these are the highest priorities. An excellent source geared to parent coaches is "Sports Psychology Basics", also available from Reedswain. It is inexpensive, complete, and yet brief. It covers the twelve most basic sports psychology concepts in a clear manner. Regarding discipline in soccer, our main concern focuses on having a menu of fun, engaging games to keep the players busy, happy and learning. This will nearly eliminate all need for disciplinary measures! Lines, long talks and sedentary activities promote discipline problems.

ADMINISTRATION and the PRESEASON TEAM MEETING

Generally it is a good idea to find someone who will do all the calling for training, cancellations, games logistics, transportation, social events, etc. Anson Dorrance, head coach of the multiple NCAA champion University of North Carolina Lady Tar Heels and former head coach of the USA Women's National Team, always mentions the importance of administration in all that he does. This is just a way of saying organization/administration is important. Still, administration can never be substituted for substance.

The only area covered in some detail here is in regard to the preseason parent meeting, which sets the tone for the whole season. First of all it should be a scheduled event in a comfortable location, usually not standing on the side of the field. Not impromptu, but with a carefully planned agenda.

Be brief, to the point and extremely informative. Too much philosophy will detract from the necessary items that follow. We'll assume for a moment that you are not an expert in the field of early childhood education, childhood sports, child psychology or the like. A simple statement that you have a child centered approach, are concerned with individual development and will attempt to find as many fun soccer learning games that teach the game should be your main emphasis, as opposed to a long diatribe of philosophy.

Do cover each of these fundamental and practical areas:
* Guidelines for attendance and being on time
* Car pooling
* Training and game locations
* Game schedule
* Field equipment tasks
* Shin guards
* Ball requirements---inflated, correct size, decent quality
* Uniforms
* Hydration needs (water bottles)
* Weather policies
* Cancellation methods
* Roster and phone chains (somewhat obsolete in the computer age, but still may be necessary)
* First aid
* Finances

- Awards
- Tournaments
- Socials
- Sportsmanship
- League rules

Cheering should be defined. Calling out a player's name during the game is not cheering, it is coaching and is not the role of the parent spectator. Calling out instructions to any child with the ball definitely interferes with their play and also is coaching, not cheering. All in all, adult responsible behavior is expected so that all may enjoy the game, especially the children. The ride home is not an interrogation period, but a period for the child to enjoy the contest he just participated in.

With a well planned written agenda there should be adequate time to cover all the items listed and still have 10-15 minutes of questions.

Outline responsibilities and seek volunteers for the various tasks that must be accomplished. First aid kit, uniform distribution, socials, travel coordinator, communications especially cancellations and any other tasks you feel need to be accomplished.

All this quality administration avoids confusion, ill feelings and the necessity to admonish someone for unpleasant sideline behavior. An ounce of prevention is worth a pound of cure!

SUMMARY

While some might think that the notion of ball touches is over emphasized, let me assure that it is not. While talent and/or physical ability will allow a youngster to dominate at a very early age, at some point that ends. Even those with a modicum of talent, let's guess somewhere about 80% of any given population with numerous contacts with the ball accompanied by game experience will excel at later age levels. To put some specific numbers on it let's consider a good high school player, college player, full scholarship Division I player and a full time paid professionals' approximate ball touches needs.

Let us consider a player from age 5 to age 17. Touching the ball at practice with a coach or on their own for two days out of three for the entire year comes to about 240 days a year. Assuming missing some days, but maybe having a Saturday with friends touching the ball 1500 or even 2500 times, let's say all of that averages out to the 240 days x 800 touches equals 192,000 touches a year. Doing that for 13 years equals approximately 2,500,00 touches. Assuming a year of injury time take away 200,000 touches. So we have 2,300,000 touches. The youngster with a modicum of talent will probably be much better than the very talented youngster with 1,000,000 ball touches. To achieve 800 touches takes less than an hour when a player is alone with the ball. Actually an hour would likely have well over 2000 ball contacts. In a training session environment it probably takes 1½ hours for about 800 ball touches. Using 1½ hours for the 2,300,000 is nearly 5000 hours, this is still far away from Daniel Coyle's seminal work in the book "The Talent Code" of 10,000 hours required for expert performance. Even assuming he over estimated the necessary time it is likely that 7000 hours is a minimal for high level for expertise in a given field. This would amount to approximately 5,000,000 touches in countless varied environments to achieve professional soccer status. And in fact, numerous professional soccer players say that they touched the ball for far more than 360 hours a year! If far more means 770 hours a year then "The Talent Code" is right on the money.

Let's forget about all the conjecturing mathematics, but one thing is very clear; that it takes millions of ball touches to reach high level performance in the game of soccer.

Even a good high school player will require a couple million touches, our Division I scholarship player maybe 3 million or more touches, and our professional player maybe 4 or 5 million or more. Naturally all of this is somewhat affected by quality of coaches encountered, levels of competition played, challenge level offered by teammates, talent, number and degree of injuries and probably several other factors. But what does not seem to change is the necessity of required ball touches for high level competence. This is enormously affected by the individual player's taking ownership of her game in order to achieve the high number of ball touches required for high level play.

Joe kicking the ball against the kicking wall!!! That's how you get to the millions of touches instead of a few hundred thousand!!!

Helping a youngster become a complete player means introducing simple basic tactics to create excitement which motivates the child to touch the ball more often and thereby refine their technical skills. The idea that we can without engaging the mind have a youngster constantly work on technical exercises that require enormous repetition makes it difficult to motivate the child, that is, allow his mind to develop along with his technical skills. Many coaches of older players seem to think that once a player is somewhat technically sound he/she will be a good player. Unfortunately many astute experienced coaches of soccer have seen technically sound players who in game situations are ineffective. They are poor players because they do not know when or where to pass, shoot, dribble or whatever is right for the game situation they find themselves in.

Introducing simple tactical concepts with the restricted games and finishing the session with free play, an unrestricted game is an absolute necessity. The competitive shortsided games that engage abundant use of technique in fun games that require some thought avoids having a youngster be a technique junkie who is ineffective in a game. Team tactics of eleven aside is of course often overdone and dangerous. But individual and two man combinations listed earlier are a necessity for developing a well rounded player. These will lead to the third man-on tactics which makes the game exciting, fun and leads to true total soccer player who is not only technically sound but shows an understanding of the game that allows them to be an asset to any team. Naturally that is the eventual goal of player development.

This is precisely why some years ago the terminology of technical/tactical came into prominence. Both the United States Soccer Federation and National Soccer Coaches Association began to understand the integral relationship between technical skills and tactical decision making.

It is unthinkable to think that the children will have fun, learn soccer and grow as healthy human beings while the coach is doing drudgery work. Simply stated the coach must enjoy the process in order to accomplish worthy goals with youngsters. Yes, it requires work in the form of planning, clinics and learning many fun activities that teach the game, but you must find a way to have fun while acquiring those skills. All successful coaches find ways to enjoy the process whether it is humor, noting the growth of the youngsters, enjoying the relationships with children and parents, or some other manner to maintain their coaching interest. Few people continue in activities that are not enjoyable to them.

Hopefully you have learned a few activities, coaching methods and ideas that will increase your players' interest in soccer. Your interaction with the content is extremely important for you to garner the maximum value from the text. In any case it was an honor to share my experience with novice coaches who devote so much time to the growth of our young soccer players.

Too often one hears all the coach does is have the players scrimmage. In actuality, generally there is inadequate amount of simple unrestricted playing of shortsided games. Many wonderful creative players have developed from touching the ball on their own and playing the game with friends at many less than ideal fields. However, this occurs less than it did in previous generations, consequently instruction has become more prominent. None-the-less simply playing is likely still the most powerful format for developing players in sport. Moderation between structured exercises, structured play and free play generally maximizes young players development of skill and passion for their sport.

The overused adage of, "No laps, no lines, no lectures" still holds merit.

If there are multiple coaches, use them! Individual instruction, bits of functional training, goalkeeping instruction and many more things are accomplished with multiple coaches. Not least is first aid, no loss of time from spontaneous needs, including TLC required for the very youngest players.

Enjoy the journey. Your biggest rewards are far in the future. When one of your former 10 year old players bumps into you at age 20 and has a glitter in his or her eye as though you were someone very special you'll know all your efforts were greatly appreciated!

www.ingramcontent.com/pod-product-compliance
Lightning Source LLC
LaVergne TN
LVHW061223060426
835509LV00012B/1397